AL–QAEDA'S RESURGENCE IN IRAQ: A THREAT TO U.S. INTERESTS

HEARING

BEFORE THE

COMMITTEE ON FOREIGN AFFAIRS
HOUSE OF REPRESENTATIVES

ONE HUNDRED THIRTEENTH CONGRESS

SECOND SESSION

FEBRUARY 5, 2014

Serial No. 113–116

Printed for the use of the Committee on Foreign Affairs

Available via the World Wide Web: http://www.foreignaffairs.house.gov/ or
http://www.gpo.gov/fdsys/

U.S. GOVERNMENT PRINTING OFFICE

86–588PDF   WASHINGTON : 2014

For sale by the Superintendent of Documents, U.S. Government Printing Office
Internet: bookstore.gpo.gov   Phone: toll free (866) 512–1800; DC area (202) 512–1800
Fax: (202) 512–2104   Mail: Stop IDCC, Washington, DC 20402–0001

CONTENTS

AL–QAEDA'S RESURGENCE IN IRAQ: A THREAT TO U.S. INTERESTS

WEDNESDAY, FEBRUARY 5, 2014

House of Representatives,
Committee on Foreign Affairs,
Washington, DC.

The committee met, pursuant to notice, at 10:07 a.m., in room 2172 Rayburn House Office Building, Hon. Edward Royce (chairman of the committee) presiding.

Chairman ROYCE. This hearing will come to order.

This morning we consider al-Qaeda's resurgence in Iraq. An unfortunate reality is that al-Qaeda in Iraq, now known as the Islamic State of Iraq and the Levant, or ISIS as you see it in the papers, is growing steadily in size, it's growing steadily in power and influence and its militant ranks have blossomed.

Last summer, ISIS carried out attacks on two different prisons in Iraq and in those attacks freed hundreds of experienced al-Qaeda fighters and leaders. The group is now able to carry out approximately 40 mass casualty attacks every month.

Multiple car bombings struck the capital this morning. The nearly 9,000 deaths in Iraq last year made it the bloodiest since U.S. forces departed in 2011.

The civil war in neighboring Syria only further strengthens this group. Militants are able to flow freely between Iraq and Syria, providing ISIS an advantage as it works to advance its regional vision of a radical Islamist state.

Their gains have been dramatic. Last month, these fighters took advantage of a security vacuum in Anbar Province, entering the cities of Fallujah and Ramadi in columns of trucks mounted with heavy machine guns and raising the black flag over government buildings.

Of course, Anbar Province is where U.S. Marines fought so hard to push out al-Qaeda. In recognizing those and other great sacrifices, I should note that this committee benefits from the first-hand experiences of Mr. Kinzinger, Mr. Cotton, Mr. Perry, Mr. DeSantis, Mr. Collins and Ms. Gabbard, all of whom served with distinction in Iraq.

This threat is evolving. Earlier this week, al-Qaeda's central leadership declared that those operating in western Iraq and Syria were no longer an affiliated group.

We will see how this power struggle develops, but ISIS' independence is a reflection of its unprecedented resources, including

(1)

weapons and personnel and cash and its resulting operational strength.

This is a threat to Iraq but also to us. ISIS has reportedly been actively recruiting individuals capable of travelling to the U.S. to carry out attacks here.

While al-Qaeda in Iraq has been powered by prison breaks and by the Syrian civil war, it has also been fuelled by the alienation of much of the Sunni population from the Shi'a dominated government in Baghdad. Al-Qaeda has become very skilled at exploiting this sectarian rift and Maliki's power grab has given them much ammunition.

This is a point that Ranking Member Eliot Engel and myself raised and underscored with President Maliki when he visited Washington last fall.

This committee will play a central role as the United States moves to send military equipment to help the Iraqis fight these terrorists. Appropriate intelligence can be shared as well.

But Iraqis should know that their relations with Iran and the slow pace of political reconciliation with minority groups raise serious congressional concerns.

While we may not be—as head of state, while he may not be up to it, Maliki must take steps to lead Iraq to a post-sectarian era. The Iraqi Government is far from perfect and only the Iraqis can control their future.

But if we don't want to see an Iraq with large swaths of territory under militant control, and we should not, then we must be willing to lend an appropriate hand.

And I'll now turn to the ranking member, Mr. Engel, for any opening comments. Mr. Engel from New York.

Mr. ENGEL. Thank you very much, Mr. Chairman.

Thank you for holding this important hearing on al-Qaeda's resurgence in Iraq and the threat this poses to U.S. security interests. I appreciate the close collaboration that we have working on this and so many other issues on this committee.

Last month, al-Qaeda extremists occupied the city of Fallujah and parts of Ramadi in Iraq's Sunni-dominated Anbar Province. To be sure, this has serious implications for Iraq's security but it also has a deeper, symbolic meaning for Americans.

As all of us know, U.S. Marines fought two bloody battles to secure Fallujah during the Iraq war. I want to acknowledge our brave men and women in uniform who lost their lives, as well as their families who continue to grieve their losses every day. It breaks my heart when I see what's happening in Iraq today.

Iraq continues to be ravaged by sectarian violence and the situation is getting worse. Last year, more than 8,500 Iraqis were killed in bombings, shootings and other violent acts, the most since 2008.

I should note that on Monday of this week, the senior leadership of al-Qaeda excommunicated and disowned their affiliate, the Islamic State of Iraq and Syria, ISIS, as a result of that group's tactics in Syria. For the purpose of this hearing, ISIS remains a threat to stability in Fallujah, other areas of Anbar Province and the whole of Iraq.

Some may argue that the lack of an enduring U.S. troop presence in Iraq has contributed to the resurgence of violence, especially Sunni terrorism related to al-Qaeda.

But let's be honest. The dire security situation in Anbar Province is much more about Iraqi politics than it is about the United States.

In any case, the direct use of U.S. military force in Iraq is virtually unthinkable at this point. We've withdrawn from Iraq and we aren't going back. Although we no longer have boots on the ground, however, the U.S. does maintain a huge stake in Iraq's security, and I believe we should continue to provide appropriate assistance to the Iraqi military in their fight against ISIS.

But we must also recognize that the current situation in Anbar cannot be resolved through military means alone. An all-out assault on Fallujah by the Iraqi security forces would play right into hands of ISIS, reinforcing the perception among Sunnis that they have been systematically victimized by Prime Minister Maliki's Shia-led government.

To defeat al-Qaeda, the Iraqi Government must take a page out of our play book from the Iraq war and enlist moderate Sunni tribes in the fight. I understand that Vice President Biden recently discussed this issue with Prime Minister Maliki, encouraging him to incorporate tribal militias fighting ISIS into the Iraqi security forces and to compensate those injured and killed in battle.

By taking these steps, I am hopeful that Maliki can begin to bridge the widening sectarian gulf in Iraq. The deterioration of Iraq's control over Anbar is also linked to larger regional dynamics.

We saw how al-Qaeda in Iraq expanded its franchise into Syria, and we now see violence from that brutal war spilling back into Iraq. This has strengthened ISIS and served as a recruitment vehicle for thousands of foreign fighters.

The slow bleed in Syria has been a clear hindrance to progress in Iraq. Iran's nefarious influence in the region also contributes to instability. It is well known that some senior Iraqi officials have a very cozy relationship with Iran, and Iraq has not done nearly enough to prevent Iranian overflights that deliver weapons to Hezbollah and the Assad regime in Syria.

In order to stabilize Iraq, the Iraqi Government will need to be a more responsible actor in the region. Chairman Royce and I made that—emphasized that point when we met with Mr. Maliki several months ago.

The discussion today is important to understand how we can encourage a political solution in Iraq that will give Sunnis a meaningful stake in the future of their country. This is the only viable way to build a safer future for Iraq while helping to curb Iranian influence and hopefully reducing the violence in Syria.

I'd like to thank Deputy Assistant Secretary Brett McGurk, one of the foremost experts on Iraq, for being here today to address these issues with us.

Mr. McGurk, I look forward to your testimony and our discussion. I yield back, Mr. Chairman.

Chairman ROYCE. Thank you, Mr. Engel. We'll hear for a minute from Ileana Ros-Lehtinen, chair of the Middle East Subcommittee, followed by Mr. Ted Deutch, who is the ranking member of that subcommittee.

Ms. ROS-LEHTINEN. Thank you very much, Mr. Chairman, and in addition to the biggest issue, which is that we don't have al-Qaeda on the run, there are two issues which I continue to be very concerned about.

First, is the safety of the residents of Camp Liberty. They still have very little protection. When last you testified, Mr. McGurk, 192 T-walls were up. Then the big progress supposedly is that 43 T-walls are now up in addition. This is out of 17,500 T-walls. T-walls save lives. Put them up.

Number two, the Iraqi Jewish archives—Ted Deutch and I and many other members are very concerned, don't want them to be shipped back. The Iraqi Government incorrectly states that these papers are theirs.

That is not true and we hope that you continue to work on that and the bigger issue that brings us together is that, obviously, since the departure of our troops al-Qaeda's reemergence has caused Iraq to be—to take a very worrisome turn for the worse.

We've sacrificed so much blood and treasure there to watch it descend into full sectarian violence and al-Qaeda's safe haven so we've got to rebuild our influence there.

Thank you, Mr. Chairman, for calling this hearing.

Chairman ROYCE. Thank you, Ms. Ros-Lehtinen.

We'll go to Mr. Deutch of Florida.

Mr. DEUTCH. Thank you, Mr. Chairman, and Ranking Member Engel for holding this extremely timely hearing.

Emboldened by instability within Iraq's Government in the searing conflict, al-Qaeda affiliated—the number of al-Qaeda affiliated fighters in Iraq has now reached levels not seen since 2006.

Al-Qaeda and Iraq's offshoot, the Islamic State of Iraq and Syria, is now the primary perpetrator of the worst violence, and as my colleagues have noted al-Qaeda has now disavowed the Islamic State of Iraq and Syria for its use of tactics deemed to be too violent.

Let me say that again. Al-Qaeda, one of the world's worst and most brutal terrorist groups, has disowned this group for being too extreme. I fear the siege of Anbar and Fallujah in January has definitively turned the page from simply ladling this spillover from the Syrian conflict to a full scale resurgence of terror in Iraq.

Various reports count the number killed in January at close to 1,000. I'm particularly concerned for the 140,000 who fled their homes as rockets were indiscriminately fired at needed humanitarian aid. The security risks posed by this resurgence are too great to ignore and, Deputy Assistant Secretary McGurk, I hope today you'll be able to shed light on what level of assistance we're providing the Iraqis and our comprehensive strategy to prevent the growth of the security threat.

And I look forward to that testimony and I yield back, Mr. Chairman.

Chairman ROYCE. Thank you. Thank you, Mr. Deutch.

Now, lastly, we'll go to Judge Ted Poe of Texas, chairman of the Terrorism Subcommittee, followed by Brad Sherman for a minute of California, who's the ranking member of that subcommittee.

Mr. Poe. Al-Qaeda in Iraq is back, certainly not on its last legs. The United States has paid a high price to help liberate Iraq from the menace of al-Qaeda.

It's frustrating that al-Qaeda is gaining ground back in Iraq. Al-Qaeda's resurgence is directly related to Prime Minister Maliki's mishandling of his government. Incompetence and corruption seem to be the norm.

He centralized power, alienated the Sunnis and brought back Shi'a hit squads. He has allowed Iranian-supported operatives to kill MEK Iranian dissidents now on seven occasions without consequences.

The last time you were here, Mr. McGurk, you testified before my subcommittee and Ileana Ros-Lehtinen's subcommittee. I predicted that there would be another attack.

Seven days after you testified in December, Camp Liberty was attacked again. All this chaos has created an environment ripe for al-Qaeda. Al-Qaeda is reestablishing a safe haven to plan and launch attacks outside the region.

That is a totally unacceptable trend. The question is what is the United States going to do, and I yield back the remainder of my time. Thank you.

Chairman Royce. Thank you. Mr. Sherman.

Mr. Sherman. In the 1940s, we occupied countries. No one doubted our right to occupy. We took our time, we created new governments and those governments created new societies.

At various other times we've invaded countries, achieved a limited military objective or as much as could be achieved at reasonable cost and we left. The first example of that was Thomas Jefferson's military intervention in Libya.

In Iraq and Afghanistan, we established a bad example. The world and even some in the United States doubted our right to occupy so we hastily installed Karzai in Afghanistan and in Iraq we installed a structure which is now presided over by Mr. Maliki.

It is not surprising that Afghanistan and Iraq continue to be problems since we have—we hastily handed over governance to those who are ill prepared. Iraq is not the most important Arab state strategically. It does not become more important in the future because we made a mistake in the past that cost us dearly in blood and treasure.

We should not compound that mistake. On the other hand, Iraq is important in part because of its proximity to Iran, which I believe is one of the greatest threats to our national security.

Finally, I agree with several of the prior speakers that we need to with regard to Camp Liberty and the T-walls, and I yield back.

Chairman Royce. Thank you, Mr. Sherman.

This morning we are pleased to be joined by Deputy Assistant Secretary for Iraq and Iran Mr. Brett McGurk. Prior to this current assignment, Mr. McGurk served as a special advisor to the national security staff and as senior advisor to Ambassadors Ryan Crocker, Chris Hill and James Jeffrey in Baghdad. He also served as a lead negotiator and coordinator during bilateral talks with the Iraqi Government back in 2008.

Without objection, by the way, your full prepared statement will be made part of the record and the members here will have 5 days to submit any statements or questions or any other extraneous material for the record.

And Mr. McGurk, if you would please summarize your remarks and then we'll go to questions.

STATEMENT OF MR. BRETT MCGURK, DEPUTY ASSISTANT SECRETARY FOR IRAQ AND IRAN, BUREAU OF NEAR EASTERN AFFAIRS, U.S. DEPARTMENT OF STATE

Mr. MCGURK. Thank you.

Good morning, Chairman Royce, Ranking Member Engel and members of this committee. Thank you for inviting me to discuss the situation in Iraq with a focus on al-Qaeda's primary offshoot in Iraq, the Islamic State of Iraq and the Levant, or ISIL.

My brief statement will discuss the threat from ISIL, the current situation in Ramadi and Fallujah and how we intend to help the Iraqis combat it.

ISIL is well known to us. Its former incarnation, al-Qaeda in Iraq, or AQI, was the focus of U.S. and Iraqi security efforts over many years, beginning with the rise of its first leader, Abu Musab al-Zarqawi, more than a decade ago.

Its current leader, Abu Bakr al-Baghdadi, is a designated global terrorist under U.S. law and we believe is currently based in Syria. His mission, as clearly stated in his own statements, is to carve out a zone of governing territory from Baghdad through Syria to Lebanon.

The Syria conflict over the past 2 years provide a platform for ISIL to gain resources, recruits and safe havens. While the precise number of ISIL fighters in Syria is unknown, Director of National Intelligence James Clapper last week testified that there are likely 26,000 extremist fighters in Syria, including 7,000 foreign fighters. Many of these fighters are affiliated with ISIL.

ISIL in its earlier incarnation, AQI, inflicted mass casualties attacks in Iraq over the years 2011 and 2012. It was not until early last year that we began to see a significant increase in its attacks, most notably suicide and vehicle bombs.

Suicide attacks, we assess, are nearly all attributable to ISIL and nearly all suicide bombers are foreign fighters who enter Iraq through Syria. To give one notable statistic, in November 2012 Iraq saw three suicide attacks throughout the country. In November 2013, it saw 50.

ISIL is now striking in Iraq along three main lines of operations. First, it is attacking Shi'a civilian areas in an effort to rekindle a civil war. These are the vast majority of attacks.

Second, it is attacking Sunni areas to eliminate rivals and govern territory. In one 30-day period between September and October, for example, ISIL suicide bombers attacked three small towns in Anbar Province.

Third, ISIL is now attacking the Kurds in northern Iraq and disputed boundary areas to incite ethnic tension and rest. ISIL likely staged and planned many of these attacks at remote encampments in western Iraq. The Iraqis began to spot these camps late last summer but proved unable to target them effectively due to unarmored helicopters and the lack of other necessary CT equipment which is needed to deny terrorists safe haven.

Today, thanks to close cooperation from this committee and the Congress, we've begun to address this problem, as I will discuss in more detail. By the end of last year, signature ISIL attacks, vehicle and suicide bombs matched levels not seen since the summer of 2007.

Overall, violence remains far lower mainly because Shi'a militias have yet to respond en masse to ISIL provocations. But the risks of such reprisals rise as ISIL attacks rise. Also, over the course of 2013 political instability and continuous unrest in Sunni areas enabled but did not cause ISIL's rise.

There was a protest movement that began after a number of bodyguards to former Minister of Finance Rafa al-Issawi were detained by Iraqi security forces. These protests placed on the national agenda a number of legitimate demands such as ending the process of de-Ba'athification and ensuring criminal due process.

We supported these legitimate demands and we worked with all parties to shape a package of legislation to address them, which is now pending in the Iraqi Parliament. Ongoing violence, however, has made it difficult for Shi'a and Kurdish blocs to support this package of legislation absent concessions for their own constituencies.

Over the course of the spring and into the summer, the protest movement became more militant with al-Qaeda flags spotted in protest squares. This accelerated a vicious cycle.

ISIL exploited unaddressed grievances and increasing violence but long overdue reforms further out of reach. This brings us to where we are today and how we intend to help the Iraqis fight back.

On January 1, 2014, convoys of up to 100 trucks with mounted heavy machine guns and anti-aircraft guns flying the black flag of al-Qaeda entered the central cities of Fallujah and Ramadi. They deployed to key objectives, destroyed most police stations and secured vital crossways. The police in both cities nearly disintegrated.

The domination of these central cities was a culmination of ISIL's 2013 strategy to govern territory and establish 7th century Islamic rule. In Fallujah, days after seizing central areas, ISIL declared the city part of an Islamic caliphate.

This message, however, is not popular in Anbar Province. In Ramadi, in the hours after ISIL arrived in force tribal leaders organized and asked for funds and arms from the central government to retake their streets.

The government responded with money, weapons and assurances that tribal fighters would enjoy full benefits of any soldier in the Iraqi army.

I have been to Iraq twice since the new year. In meetings with Prime Minister Maliki and other Iraqi leaders, I have pressed upon them the urgent necessity of mobilizing the population against ISIL.

I have also discussed the situation directly with tribal and local leaders in Anbar Province. These coordinated efforts have begun to produce results. Fighting continues in Ramadi's outskirts but local leaders report that the central city is increasingly secure with tribal fighters working in coordination with local leaders.

The Iraqi army has remained outside, helping where necessary to secure populated areas. The situation in Fallujah is more serious with hardened ISIL fighters and former insurgents in control of the streets. One week ago, ISIL fighters captured a group of Iraqi soldiers, paraded them around the city flying al-Qaeda's black flag and then executed them.

Further complicating the situation, we assess that some tribes in and around Fallujah are supporting ISIL while others are fighting ISIL and many others remain on the fence. The hardened fighters inside the city are seeking to draw the army into a direct confrontation.

Thus far, the army has not taken the bait, focusing its efforts on the outskirts and keeping tribal fighters in the lead. But make no mistake, the Government of Iraq, working in full coordination with local leaders and the local population, has a responsibility to secure Fallujah.

Under the plan that is now being developed as explained to us by local and national leaders late last week, tribal fighters will lead this effort with the army in support when needed.

The United States is prepared to offer advice, make recommendations and share lessons learned based on our deep experience in these areas. General Austin, in a visit to Baghdad last week, had a series of candid conversations with Iraqi officials and commanders about the importance of patience and planning.

ISIL is also planning to consolidate control of Fallujah and move 30 miles east of Baghdad. In a rare audio statement, on January 21st ISIL's leader directed his fighters "to be on the front lines against the Shi'a and march toward Baghdad."

Were there any doubt of potential risks for the United States, he added what he said was a direct message to the Americans: "Soon we will be in direct confrontation so watch for us for we are with you watching." We take such threats seriously and through cooperation with this committee and the Congress we intend to help the Iraqis in their efforts to defeat ISIL over the long term. Here's how.

First, we are pressing the national leadership in the highest possible levels to develop a holistic security political economic strategy to isolate extremists from the population. This means supporting local tribal fighters, incorporating those fighters into the security services and committing to April elections to be held on time.

Second, we are supporting the Iraqi security forces through accelerated foreign military sales, training and information sharing. The Iraqis have now equipped Caravan aircraft, for example, to fire Hellfire missiles thereby denying ISIL safe haven in the western desert.

Such assistance is offered pursuant to a holistic strategy and we've made clear to the Iraqis that security operations, while a necessary condition for defeating ISIL, are not sufficient.

Third, we are actively encouraging an aggressive economic component to mobilize the Sunni population against ISIL. In the 5 weeks since ISIL entered Ramadi and Fallujah, the GOI has allocated over $35 million to Anbar Province in assistance and payments to fighters.

Throughout, our message to all Iraqi leaders is firm. Despite your differences across a host of issues, you must find a way to work together when it comes to ISIL, an organization that threatens all Iraqis.

This is particularly true for Prime Minister Maliki who, as the head of state, must take extra measures to reach out to Sunni leaders and draw critical mass of the local population into the fight.

I want to thank you again for allowing me to address this most important topic. I look forward to working closely with you in the months ahead to protect U.S. interests in Iraq and throughout the region and I look forward to your questions.

Thank you.

[The prepared statement of Mr. McGurk follows:]

Testimony of Deputy Assistant Secretary Brett McGurk
House Foreign Affairs Committee Hearing: Iraq

February 5, 2014

Chairman Royce, Ranking Member Engel, and Members of the Committee, thank you for inviting me to discuss the situation in Iraq with a focus on al Qa'ida's primary offshoot in Iraq, the Islamic State of Iraq and the Levant (ISIL).

Threat Posed by the Islamic State of Iraq and the Levant (ISIL)

I will begin with a brief overview of the security situation in 2011 and 2012, as it is important to understanding the current environment. In both years, 2011 and 2012, Iraq remained a very violent country. By our counts, 4,400 Iraqis were killed each year, most in attacks by extremist groups led by al-Qa'ida in Iraq (AQI).

While this violence was persistent and targeted, it did not threaten the stability of the state, or a rekindled civil war. Indeed, based on studies of historical parallels – civil wars and insurgencies – Iraq by 2012 had entered what is called a "low boil" stage of insurgency. A low boil insurgency reflects a level of violence that may not present a serious risk of state collapse, or rekindled broad scale reprisals, but rather a persistent tempo of attacks carried out by the hardened core of an insurgency – which, by historical examples, can take a decade to fizzle out.

These two years, 2011 and 2012, also witnessed the escalating civil war in Syria, inflamed by regional rivalry and opportunism by terrorist groups. The Asad regime's unwillingness to engage with the opposition in meaningful political dialogue and violent suppression of peaceful protests led to open, armed conflict. As the fighting has dragged on, the conflict has attracted terrorist groups seeking to take advantage of the loss of state authority, including in eastern Syria, leading to the rise of terrorist groups near the Iraq border.

The most organized and lethal of these groups – the al-Nusrah Front and ISIL – were franchises of AQI. They vary in their objectives: al-Nusrah has put greater priority on the toppling of Asad and working with other Syrian opposition groups, whereas ISIL has focused on a more regional agenda, with an aim to carve out an Islamic caliphate stretching from Baghdad to Lebanon. These dueling objectives have at times required direct mediation by Osama Bin Laden's former deputy, and now global head of al-Qa'ida, Ayman al Zawahiri. The debate has been a central focus among global jihadist networks, and has given ISIL, in particular, a global platform to propagate its agenda and recruit adherents.

Flush with resources, recruits, weapons, and training, ISIL slowly began to execute its strategy across the Syrian border in Iraq. Violence in Iraq ticked up towards the end of 2012, but did not accelerate until early 2013. This included a marked rise in suicide bombers. The majority of these suicide bombers, we believe, are foreign fighters, recruited through extremist propaganda. Suicide bombers are a key data point we track, as they have a pernicious effect on the stability of Iraq, and demonstrate a sophisticated global network that is able to recruit, train, and deploy human beings to commit suicide and mass murder. The suicide bombers are, in a twisted turn of logic, ISIL's most precious resource.

It was significant, therefore, that by early 2013, we began to see signs of ISIL shifting these resources from Syria to Iraq. In 2012, Iraq witnessed an average of 5-10 suicide attacks per month. By the summer of 2013, it was averaging 30-40 suicide attacks per month, and increasingly coordinated and effective attacks. On March 14, 2013, for example, five suicide bombers from ISIL attacked and took hostages in the Ministry of Justice in Baghdad, and controlled the building for several hours before detonating themselves. This was the first in a series of sophisticated military-style operations throughout 2013, with suicide bombers used to clear a path, followed by well-trained fighters to take and hold an objective.

By the summer of 2013, ISIL suicide bombers struck regularly, focused primarily on Shia civilian targets (playgrounds, funerals, markets), but also Sunni areas (to contest territory) and Kurdish areas (to spark ethnic conflict). In November 2013, Iraq witnessed 50 suicide attacks, compared with only three in November 2012. These attacks had a devastating effect on political discourse in the country, further fueling mistrust from political leaders to ordinary citizens, and making the tangible reforms that Iraq needs to reconcile its society even harder to reach.

Indeed, the violence may appear indiscriminate – but it is not. From what we are now seeing, ISIL attacks are calculated, coordinated, and part of a strategic campaign led by its Syria-based leader, Abu Bakr al-Baghdadi. This campaign has the stated objective to cause the collapse of the Iraqi state and carve out a zone of governing control in the western regions of Iraq and eastern Syria (an area known as the "Jazeera"). To do this, they are now using three primary tactics:

- First, attacking Shia civilians with an aim to re-ignite a civil war and cause ordinary people to look to militias, not the state, for protection. Adherents to

ISIL's extreme ideology believe Shia should be killed based on their sect alone, and the suicide bombers seek populated areas to murder as many innocent people as possible. These are the vast majority of ISIL attacks.

- Second, contesting territory in Sunni areas to assert dominance over local Sunni officials and tribes. Targeted assassinations and attacks increased in these areas as ISIL focused its resources inside Iraq. In one 30-day period between September and October of last year, for example, more than a dozen suicide bombers were used in assaults on three towns in Anbar province (Rawa, Rutbah, and Haditha).

- Third, attacking the Iraqi Kurdistan Region (IKR) and disputed boundary areas in northern Iraq to stoke ethnic tensions and conflict. The thriving capital city of the IKR, Erbil, faced an attack in September similar to attacks seen in Baghdad earlier in the year: multiple suicide bombers followed by an infantry assault to temporarily control a government building.

By the end of 2013, suicide and vehicle-borne attacks initiated by ISIL returned to levels not seen since the height of AQI's power (its earlier incarnation) in 2007. Overall levels of violence, however, remain far below 2007 levels, demonstrating that reprisal attacks from Shia militias have been restrained, though the risks of such reprisals continue to rise as ISIL continues to attack Shia civilian areas.

In summary, ISIL's strategy is sophisticated, patient, and focused. It will take a similar combination of sophistication, patience, and focus to combat it, and I will explain shortly what this strategy should look like, and how we intend to help the Iraqis increase the chances that they can arrest these 2013 trend-lines in 2014.

Political Instability Enables ISIL Operations

The above picture would not be complete without discussing the political situation in Iraq, and how it does – and does not – impact these violence trends. Over the course of 2013, the security situation deteriorated against a backdrop of political instability and protests in Sunni areas of the country. These protests began after

Iraqi forces detained a number of bodyguards to then-Minister of Finance Rafa al-Issawi in late December 2012. Issawi later resigned from his post.[1]

The guilt or innocence of the bodyguards and their detention soon became a side issue, as the protest demands grew to encompass a full catalog of decade-long grievances among Iraq's Sunni community. These grievances included appeals to end the process of de-Ba'athfication, which began in 2003, reform the criminal procedure code to ensure due process rights to detainees, and greater power sharing in national governance decision-making and institutions.[2]

From the very beginning, participants in these protests varied: some had legitimate political demands, such as those listed above; others rejected the entire post-2003 political order and questioned the legitimacy of the state; while a small minority was openly militant and advocated violence against the central government. The latter two groups were often the most visible and vocal, which made it increasingly difficult (due to constituent pressure in some cases, excuses in others) to convince prominent Shia and Kurdish leaders to address demands from the first group.

The toxic combination of unaddressed grievances and rising terrorist attacks created a pressure cooker with no safety valve, and ISIL took advantage. Its black flags began to appear at protest squares, particularly in Fallujah, further alienating the Shia population and fueling the charged sectarian environment. In April, Iraqi forces moved to clear one of the most militant protest squares, in the north-central town of Hawija. The operation appears to have begun peacefully, but shots were later exchanged, followed by a barrage, leaving nearly 50 people dead.

After that incident, some Sunni nationalist insurgent groups, including Jaysh Rijal al-Tariq al-Naqshabandi (JRTN), openly vowed to attach Iraqi Security Forces (ISF) and declared a new offensive against Baghdad. The JRTN is a militant

---

[1] Rafa al-Issawi has been a close partner of the United States, and we believe his official status and standing should be restored as soon as possible. I met with Issawi earlier this month and found him committed and dedicated to helping isolate and defeat ISIL in Anbar province.

[2] We fully support addressing these grievances, and have worked with all political blocs to develop a package of laws that answer legitimate demands through the political process. In April, the Iraqi cabinet approved this package of laws, including sweeping reforms to the de-Ba'athification process. The Iraqi parliament, however, has yet to take up a vote on this package. This is partially due to pressing matters in other areas (such as passing the law to govern April elections, which took months of debate) and partially due to lack of support among the Shi'a and Kurdish blocs. We continue to call on all political blocs to work together and finalize this important package of laws for an up-or-down vote.

offshoot of the Iraqi Baath party, and together with AQI, designated under U.S. law as a Foreign Terrorist Organization. Its resurgence added to the instability in Sunni areas, fueled mistrust in Shia areas, and facilitated the rise and entrenchment of ISIL, particularly in border regions of Ninewa province. Today, ISIL and JRTN appear to be working together in some areas, but with vastly different agendas – this partnership is likely to be short-lived.

The danger at this moment is that these hardened cores of militancy, which must be isolated from the broader population and defeated, become fused with a sense of despondency and grievance in Sunni areas of the country. It is therefore critical and incumbent upon the Government of Iraq (GOI) to help mobilize the people in Sunni areas against ISIL and JRTN through a combination of aggressive political outreach and targeted intelligence-driven security operations.

This responsibility for political outreach and inclusion rests on all Iraqi leaders, but most prominently on Prime Minister Nouri al-Maliki. He is under tremendous political pressure from the Shia population, which faces a near daily threat of car and suicide bombs; but it is incumbent upon the head of state to act in a manner that advances stability in all parts of Iraq. In all of our engagements with Maliki, accordingly, including a November meeting with the President, and regular calls from the Vice President, we have continued to press the urgency of working with local Sunni leaders to draw the population into the fight against ISIL.

The Current Situation: Fallujah and Ramadi

On January 1, 2014, convoys of approximately 70-100 trucks with mounted heavy weapons and anti-aircraft guns, flying the black flag of al-Qa'ida, entered the central cities of Fallujah and Ramadi. They deployed to key objectives, destroyed most police stations, and secured vital crossways. The police in both cities nearly disintegrated. The Iraqi army, deployed in camps outside the cities, engaged some armed vehicles but generally chose not to get drawn into urban fighting.

The domination of these central cities was a culmination of ISIL's 2013 strategy to govern territory and establish 7th-century Islamic rule. Across the border in Syria, ISIL has governed the city of Raqqa (with a population of 220,000) for most of the past year. In Iraq, ISIL sees Ramadi and Fallujah as their new Raqqa. In Fallujah, days after seizing central areas, ISIL declared the city part of an Islamic caliphate. This message, however, is not popular in Anbar – and has bred fierce resistance.

In Ramadi, in the hours after ISIL arrived in force, tribal leaders organized and asked for funding and arms from the central government to retake their streets and protect their population. The GOI responded with $17 million to support urgent humanitarian assistance and reconstruction of areas damaged in fighting. It also began sending small and medium weapons to tribal fighters, with assurance that these fighters would be given full benefits of the state, as if they were soldiers.

I was in Iraq in early January as this effort got underway. In meetings with Maliki and other key leaders, I pressed the urgent message that without a broad base of support from the population in Ramadi, it would be impossible to root out the hundreds of ISIL fighters who had taken up positions in strategic areas. I also discussed the situation with former leaders of the Anbar awakening, such as Sheikh Abu Risha, and local officials in Ramadi, including Governor Ahmed Khalaf, who were focused on organizing tribal fighters to oust ISIL from populated areas.

Over the first two weeks of January, these local and tribal leaders made requests to the central government for additional resources, weapons, and a common strategy to reclaim the streets from ISIL and other militant groups. The GOI dispatched the acting Defense Minister, Sadoun Dulaimi, to fulfill these requests and finalize a military and political plan. (Dulaimi is from Anbar and a member of one of its largest tribes. He has been in Ramadi nearly full-time since this crisis began.)

These coordinated efforts have begun to produce results. Fighting continues in the outskirts of Ramadi, but the central city is increasingly secure with a critical mass of tribes having pledged to fight ISIL to ensure that they cannot return. This quick albeit fragile turnaround in Ramadi, with serious and regular coordination between local and national leaders, may provide a model for how we can best ensure that 2014 is a year in which the tide begins to turn once again against ISIL inside Iraq.

The Fallujah situation is far more serious, as hundreds of ISIL fighters have joined ranks with former insurgent groups to consolidate control of the inner city, and contest areas in small towns nearby. The Iraqi army is now working to establish a cordon from the outskirts of the city, in coordination with local tribes, but they face well-trained snipers armed with 50-caliber rifles. On January 26, approximately a dozen Iraqi soldiers were captured near Fallujah. Some were later paraded around the city in the back of a pickup truck flying the al-Qa'ida flag. The next day, ISIL posted a video showing their gruesome execution, daring the army to enter the city.

The army, thus far, has not taken the bait. It remains on the city's outskirts, working to execute a strategy similar to what proved effective in Ramadi. There had been reports of army units randomly shelling Fallujah's neighborhoods, but

Iraqi commanders have denied this (blaming ISIL), and tribal figures have since confirmed that military operations are being coordinated with local actors.

At this moment, Fallujah is the scene of a tense standoff. Some tribes are ready and preparing to fight ISIL, others are working with ISIL (and forming "tribal councils" with declared intention to fight the army), and more are on the fence, waiting to see which side is likely to prevail in the end. Local leaders in Anbar, in coordination with the GOI, are working to recruit more tribes to enter, clear, and hold Fallujah, while ensuring civilians and families can leave the city.

This standoff will not last forever. The GOI has the responsibility to help local leaders secure the city and oust the militants now in control. Under the plan that is being developed by the GOI in coordination with local leaders, the army will seek to control outlying areas and cordon the city; tribal fighters will then seek to take the lead in securing populated areas, with military support when needed. We know from experience how difficult this will be, and U.S. military officers from the Office of Security Cooperation are in regular touch with their Iraqi counterparts to share lessons learned, offer advice, and make recommendations.

ISIL has also made its intentions clear: move from a new base of operations in Fallujah to Baghdad – a distance of under 30 miles. Its leader, Abu Bakr al-Baghdadi, had this to say in a rare audio statement issued on January 21:

> "As for ISIS in Iraq: Be in the frontlines against the Shia, and march toward Baghdad and the South, keep the Shia busy in their own areas. Know that the entire Sunni population and the brothers in Syria are watching you."

Were there any doubt, moreover, of the threat Baghdadi and his network – now with approximately 2,000 fighters in Iraq – presents to the United States and our interests in the region, his statement said this in its concluding paragraph:

> "Our last message is to the Americans. Soon we will be in direct confrontation, and the sons of Islam have prepared for such a day. So watch, for we are with you, watching."

Developing a Long-Term Iraqi Strategy: Political, Economic, Security

Drawing on our own lessons learned, we are also encouraging the GOI to develop and execute a holistic strategy to isolate and defeat ISIL over the long-term. This strategy fuses political, security, and economic components with an immediate focus on incorporating tribal fighters to protect the population in towns and villages throughout the provinces of Anbar, Ninewa, and Sal ah Din. These tribal fighters would work in coordination with local officials, local police, and the army when needed, to deny space and sanctuary for an organized ISIL presence.

Such a strategy is extremely difficult to develop and execute in a dynamic tribal environment like Anbar province. But in recent weeks, we have seen a new level of commitment from the GOI to mobilize the local population against ISIL. Over the course of January, the GOI cabinet has allocated resources to ensure local people taking up arms against extremist groups enjoy full state benefits in the event they are killed or wounded. Importantly, the GOI has committed to incorporating these fighters into the security structures of the state once fighting concludes.

Regarding economic support, in January alone, the GOI allocated $18 million for rebuilding projects in Fallujah and Ramadi; $17 million for direct humanitarian assistance; and $3.4 million for direct payments to tribal fighters. As noted above, Sadoun Dulaimi has remained in Ramadi to oversee allocation of these resources. Our team in Baghdad is in direct and regular contact with all relevant actors, and urging them to ensure resources reach intended recipients as soon as possible.

In my own visits to Baghdad last month, including one just last week, I found the national leadership increasingly attuned to the necessity of enlisting popular support as a necessary condition for defeating ISIL. I also detected, for the first time, acknowledgement that GOI missteps over the course of 2013 may have made the situation worse, and that this coming year must be different in terms of strategy and execution. As the GOI spokesman told the *Washington Post* last week:

> "We are supplying [the tribes] with more weapons and whatever they need. They will be treated like any troop in the Iraqi army. They will have salaries and pensions and any right a troop in the Iraqi army has."

This statement articulates precisely what must be done, and fairly reflects my own hard conversations with local and national leaders over this past month.

Finally, at the national political level, we are focused on ensuring that the political process remains on track, most importantly with national elections on April 30th. More than forty coalitions have registered to compete in these elections, which will choose a parliament to form a new government to serve through 2018.

One cannot overstate the importance of these elections, and we have made clear to all Iraqi leaders that they must happen on time, with oversight by the Independent

High Electoral Commission (IHEC) and the United Nations Mission in Iraq (UNAMI). The work by IHEC and UNAMI, thus far, has been heroic, and we will continue to support their missions between now and Election Day.

Security Measures (and focused U.S. Support)

Political and economic initiatives are necessary for defeating a network like ISIL. But they are not sufficient. From our own experience, we know that while success is impossible without mobilizing the population, such popular mobilization will not last absent focused and persistent security operations. The tribes will fight, but they must be confident that they are going to win and be recognized when the fighting is over – not left to the mercy of ISIL reprisals. For this to happen, ISIL networks must be constantly pressured, and their safe havens destroyed.

Consistent with ISIL's rise last summer, a series of armed camps – staging areas and training grounds – were spotted in western Iraq. The existence of these camps demonstrated a shortfall in the capacity of the ISF. Even where camps could be located, through persistent ISF reconnaissance platforms, such as manned King Air platforms, the ISF lacked the ability to target effectively, thereby providing ISIL safe haven just miles from populated areas.

Iraq's lack of armored helicopters was a glaring example. Iraqi pilots, over the course of 2013, often flew thin-skinned helicopters towards ISIL camps defended by PKC machine guns and anti-aircraft platforms. The result was helicopters shot up and crews (many of whom we had trained) suffering grievous wounds. This situation was not sustainable, and the GOI requested our urgent assistance.

I want to thank this Committee, in particular, for working so closely with us over the past six months to approve the Apache helicopter lease and sale through our Foreign Military Sales program. While this is not an immediate remedy to the current problem, they will provide the ISF with the most effective platform possible for denying ISIL a safe haven in the remote western deserts of Iraq. They will also ensure that we can provide effective oversight on the end use of attack helicopter systems, as well as influencing planning and operations.

Similarly, the Iraqis have recently proven effective at deploying Hellfire missiles against remote ISIL targets from a Caravan aircraft. The ISF have equipped Caravans to launch Hellfire strikes, but the overall supply of Hellfire missiles was not adequate to tackle the threat and number of targets they had located and surveyed. Again, thanks to close coordination with this Committee, this situation has begun to change. We delivered 75 Hellfire missiles in December, and have notified Congress of a potential sale of up to 500 more. Our objective is to ensure that ISIL can never again gain safe haven in western Iraq.

Consistent with this strategy, we will deliver 10 Scan Eagle surveillance UAVs this spring, and 48 Raven UAVs later this year, all of which, when used in combination with other platforms, can provide regular surveillance of the Jazeera region and the Iraq-Syria border. As Director of National Intelligence Clapper noted in recent testimony before the Senate Select Committee on Intelligence, the "greater two way flow of Sunni extremists between Syria and Iraq" has a direct bearing on ISIL's ability to conduct high-profile attacks in Iraq. To be successful, thus, a long-term strategy must focus on security and surveillance in these areas.

Finally, we have increased bilateral and regional training opportunities for Iraqi counterterrorism (CT) units, and expedited deliveries of key CT-related equipment for Iraq's most elite and disciplined units. U.S. trainers with the Embassy's Office of Security Cooperation are also conducting non-operational training with these high-end Iraqi operators, and Iraq and Jordan have discussed the possibility of advanced training for Iraqi forces in Jordan. We fully support this initiative.

All of this assistance comes in the context of the holistic strategy discussed above, short of which, long-term stability will not be possible. This was a point General Austin pressed home with Prime Minister Maliki and other key leaders in a visit to Baghdad last week: security, economics, and politics, must be fused together.

***

Before concluding, I would like to say a brief word to our men and women who served so bravely in these areas of Iraq. I cannot imagine what it must have been like to see al-Qa'ida raise its flag once again in the cities of Fallujah and Ramadi. I was sickened by the spectacle. But I want to ensure everyone who served, and this Committee, that we will do everything possible to help the Iraqis take back their streets. The situation in Ramadi is slowly improving, and we will support the Iraqis – and the tribes of Anbar province – to secure the city of Fallujah.

Conclusion

Vital U.S. interests are at stake in Iraq. While my testimony today has focused on the threat from ISIL, the issues of oil, regional stability, and Iranian influence, are also central to our policy during this pivotal new year. I look forward to working closely with this Committee to ensure that we are doing all we can to protect and advance U.S. interests month-to-month. Thank you again for the opportunity to address these complex issues today. I look forward to answering your questions.

————

Chairman ROYCE. Thank you, Mr. McGurk.

The first question I was going to ask you related to something that happened last summer. There were militant camps and training grounds spotted in western Iraq.

So we could see this brewing, and yesterday we heard the CIA Director note before Congress that there are camps inside of both Iraq and Syria that are, in his words, used by al-Qaeda to develop capabilities that are applicable both in theater as well as beyond.

So you noted that the Iraqi Government could spot these camps but did not have the ability to target effectively, leaving safe havens just miles from populated areas, in your words.

If these al-Qaeda camps present a direct threat to our interests and the Iraqis can't deal with it, then why weren't we doing more against these camps?

You know, how would this gap that the Iraqi capabilities obviously can't meet be closed? How could you effectively move on this?

Mr. McGurk. Thank you, Mr. Chairman.

Let me kind of walk through the last 4 or 5 months. Really, late last summer the Iraqis spotted some of these camps and they tried to target them. They flew Bell 104 helicopters out—47 helicopters out there.

The helicopters were shot up by PKC machine guns. They tried to send the army out there. The army was IED'd on the roads, which are heavily booby trapped. So it was pretty clear that despite a very strong Iraqi security force capability they were not able to target camps in these remote areas and their special forces also could not operate effectively in those areas.

And that is when we began to accelerate some of our foreign military assistance programs and also information sharing to get a better intelligence picture. So two notable developments over recent months.

First, the Iraqis have become very effective with the Hellfire missile strikes through their Caravan aircrafts and we are helping them in the find, fix and finish mission in which they're undertaking, and second, we believe, as we've had many discussions with this committee—many good discussions—that Apache helicopter platforms are really a critical platform for denying safe haven in these areas over the long term, and I want to thank this committee for helping us with that sale, which was recently approved.

But this won't be immediate. It won't be until later this year that the first leased helicopters get into the country and are operational. But that is really a long-term solution to this problem.

Chairman ROYCE. The other question I was going to ask you was in your testimony you called suicide bombers a key data point we track and noted that these suicide bombers operating in Iraq are in fact foreign fighters that have come in.

Where are these foreign fighters coming from? We've seen reports that close to a 1,000 have come from Europe, some from the U.S. I was going to ask you how do you assess the threat to U.S. personnel, not only that threat to personnel and our interests in the region but also here in the United States.

Mr. McGurk. Mr. Chairman, the foreign fighters in Syria are coming from all over the world. This is a problem we faced in the years 2006 to 2008 when foreign fighters were coming into Syria and also making their way into Iraq through what was then the al-Qaeda in Iraq network.

They're coming mainly from the region. But we do assess from our best intelligence assessments that the suicide bombers are foreign fighters. Right now, they do not pose a direct threat to us or our personnel but they pose a direct threat to the stability of Iraq.

The suicide bombers, and again, about five to 10 a month over 2011 and 2012, now about 30 to 40 a month, it has a pernicious effect on the political discourse in the country.

Car bombs—the Iraqis have been able to protect against car bombs. You don't see mass casualty car bomb attacks like you used to see. There are still a lot of car bombs but casualties are lower.

It's the suicide bombers that are able to get into funerals, mosques, populated areas and cause mass casualties, which has just a devastating effect on the country. So it's a very serious, serious problem and a regional problem.

Chairman ROYCE. And the last question I'll ask in my remaining moments, you were just in Baghdad meeting with Iraqi officials and you state that you detected for the first time acknowledgment that Government of Iraq missteps may have made the problem worse, and as I noted in my statement this is not the feeling that Ranking Member Engel and I received when we raised this issue with the President of Iraq in our meeting. So that was a few months ago.

I am somewhat encouraged by this but how encouraged should we be? Because our concern has long been that this lack of reconciliation is compounding the problem seriously.

Mr. MCGURK. I have found, frankly, Mr. Chairman, an attitude among the Iraqis that was similar to the tactics that we used in the early part of the war, that the security problem was simply a security problem and not a problem that was fused with politics and economics, and we had a series of conversations over the course of last year as the ISIL attacks increased in which Iraqis saw this mainly as a security problem.

All I can say is that I've been there twice this month since the entry of ISIL into Fallujah and Ramadi and I have heard from across the board from the Prime Minister on down that unless you enlist local Sunnis in those areas you will never defeat and isolate ISIL.

And we have seen that now manifested in a commitment. The Iraqi cabinet has passed a number of resolutions saying tribal fighters will be given full benefits of the state and, most significantly, Prime Minister Maliki has made a commitment that tribal fighters who oust ISIL from these areas will be incorporated into the formal security services of the state—the police and the army.

That did not happen with the Awakening fighters that we worked with in 2006 to 2008. So that is a very significant commitment. We now need to stay on the Iraqis to make sure they follow through.

Chairman ROYCE. Thank you. We'll go to Mr. Engel.

Mr. ENGEL. Thank you, Mr. Chairman.

Mr. McGurk, let me ask you about al-Qaeda in Iraq. It's been reported that al-Zawahiri, the head of al-Qaeda, has disowned the Islamic State of Iraq and Syria. So if that's true, what does that mean for al-Qaeda's presence in Iraq?

What are the repercussions for ISIS operating without the al-Qaeda umbrella and how will this affect the rebel infighting in Syria now that al-Nusra has the blessing of al-Qaeda?

Mr. McGurk. Well, ISIL and al-Nusra were both kind of—came out of al-Qaeda in Iraq. ISIL basically is al-Qaeda in Iraq. Its leader was the al-Qaeda in Iraq leader since 2010.

Nusra was a bit of an offshoot and is focused more on Syria. As you said, there's now this message, which seems from Zawahiri, saying that ISIL is no longer affiliated with al-Qaeda central.

I would defer to my intelligence colleagues on the long-term effects but what we have found is that ISIL has such a media presence, such a propaganda presence and is able to self-sustain itself by controlling facilities in eastern Syria including oil facilities and also through extortion rackets in cities in western Iraq that it'll be able to maintain its cycle of operations.

In terms of those who are recruited and come in to ISIL, it's really—their message, and it goes all the way back to Zarqawi 10 years ago, is just very perniciously sectarian, that Shi'a Muslims in particular simply don't have a right to live and they should be killed, and those who believe that tend to gravitate toward ISIL.

Nusra is more of a al-Qaeda central-like message and also including a threat to us. But I think—despite this new statement we've seen I think ISIL is going to maintain its pace of operations and continue to be a very serious threat.

Mr. Engel. Thank you.

I'd like to ask you some questions about Iraq and Iran and the relationship. When I look back at the war in Iraq, what really breaks my heart is that we lost so many Americans, so much American blood, and now it's almost as if we didn't do anything.

Nothing we did was positive. It's all been eroded, and it really just breaks my heart for people who lost loved ones there.

We're the ones responsible, in my opinion, for making Iran the hegemonic power in the region because Iran and Iraq for years fought wars, checked each other and once we blew up—not that Saddam Hussein was worth anything but once we blew up the minority Sunni regime in Iraq and it seems to me it was only obvious that the Shi'as in Iraq would gravitate to the Shi'as in Iran, and the sad thing is that Iran has more influence, in my opinion, in Iraq now than we have.

So there are reports, and Chairman Royce and I raised this with Mr. Maliki when he was in Washington, that Iraq is allowing Iran overflights as Iran seeks to arm Hezbollah. Hezbollah, obviously, is now fighting the war in Syria on Assad's side. It's helping Hezbollah expand its presence in Syria, defending the Assad regime.

So can you characterize that relationship that Prime Minister Maliki and other senior Iraqi officials have with Iran and how would you describe Iraq's commitments to the U.S. on the over-flight issue? Does Maliki understand how this destabilizes the region?

Mr. MCGURK. Iraq's relationship with Iran is multifaceted. We have found repeatedly over the years that Iraq acts primarily in its own interests.

We found very few instances in which we've seen Iraq acting at the behest of Iran in which it did not see it acting in its own interests. You can look at that in terms of Iraq's overall oil production. You can look at it in terms of Iraq ratifying the additional protocol.

You can look at it in terms of Iraq supporting the Geneva 1 communique, a number of steps in which we know the Iranians were pressing the Iraqis not to do things and the Iraqis did them. The issue of overflights is something where the Iraqis have not done enough. We have seen the number of flights come down.

We continue to press this issue. Inspections go up. Inspections go down. It's very frustrating. It's often very difficult for us to get a precise intelligence picture of specific flights and what's on a flight.

We know that material, we believe, is coming on civilian aircraft. So it's just—it's a problem that we focus on all the time. It's the one area where I can say Iraq is simply not doing enough.

Mr. ENGEL. I just—thank you. I just want to make one final comment and that it's—it was my opinion when the chairman and I met with Mr. Maliki that he was a good listener but I didn't think he provided too much in terms of answers to the questions we had, one of which was overflights.

I think that he just came to listen but, really, didn't come to put his head together with us and help solve the problem.

Mr. MCGURK. I have found, Congressmen, that the—since the Prime Minister's trip that your meeting with him, other meetings he had here on the Hill, he spent about 2 hours with President Obama in the Oval Office, he got a very direct message on a number of issues and we have seen some fairly significant changes from that visit.

So I want to thank you for the meeting you had with him. I think you made an influence. On some of the issues which I know were discussed with Camp Liberty we've seen some changes, and particularly in the need for a holistic strategy to defeat ISIL and enlisting the Sunnis into the fight at the local level we have seen some fairly dramatic and significant changes from that visit.

Mr. ENGEL. Thank you. Thank you, Mr. Chairman.

Chairman ROYCE. Thank you, Mr. Engel.

We go now to Ileana Ros-Lehtinen.

Ms. ROS-LEHTINEN. Thank you so much, Mr. Chairman.

Welcome once again, sir. The Iraqi Jewish archives—you have been engaged in discussions with the Iraqis on this issue and your staff has spoken to—with representatives of the Iraqi Jewish Diaspora and the Jewish community as a whole.

But could you give us an update on progress of these discussions? Have there been alternative plans proposed? On the issue of the T-walls at Camp Liberty, why have there been only 235 out of 17,500 T-walls put up and why have we only seen an addition of 43 since our November subcommittee hearing? Can you please commit that you will put extra effort in saving lives there?

And then thirdly, as far as al-Qaeda's resurgence, a large part of this is due to the failure in the Iraqi Government and Iraqi leadership since we left the country. There are national elections planned in Iraq in April.

We were successful after the surge in getting the Iraqi Government to participate in a more inclusive power sharing government that kind of mollified the Sunnis of Iraq and left al-Qaeda marginalized. Then after we left the Iraqis took another step backward.

Now it was the Sunnis who were marginalized, drawing many of them toward al-Qaeda. What steps are we taking to ensure that the Sunnis are participating in these elections and that Iraq can return to that sort of power sharing government we saw in the post-surge Iraq?

And continuing with the Shi'a-Sunni issue we've seen over the last few days that the Iraqi military has been bombarding Fallujah, which was taken over by al-Qaeda late last year, presumably preparing the way for a ground assault.

However, the Shi'a-dominated Maliki government cannot successfully take Fallujah on its own without the help of the Sunni tribal leaders in the region. Can you describe the current—our relationship between the Maliki government and these tribal leaders and do you think Maliki will be able to gain their support, given Maliki's crackdown on Sunnis in Iraq for these past few years?

Thank you, sir.

Mr. McGurk. Thank you.

Let me take the topics in order. On the Jewish archives, as you know this is a very sensitive topic. I've been working directly with the Iraqis on this. I was just in Iraq and raised it with those officials who are charged with the file. We are engaged in sensitive negotiations with the Iraqis.

In the coming weeks, the director of Iraq's National Library and Archives will be coming to the United States and, again, I hope to report progress on this. But we're engaged and it's a sensitive negotiation but I will keep you fully informed of those talks.

On Camp Liberty, on specifically on the issue T-walls, I have, again, made a number of trips to Iraq and every time I go from Maliki on down I raise the issue of T-walls. We got T-walls moving back into the camp earlier this month. They stopped.

I raised it again last Thursday with the Iraqi national security advisor. I understand this morning T-walls are moving into the camp again. I visited the survivors and residents at Camp Liberty earlier this month. I told them I promised I would do everything I could.

I also urged them to do everything they could and that meant showing up at these camp management meetings where plans are made to move the T-walls into the camp. This is an issue I'm going to continue to stay on top of.

On the issue of elections and Sunni participation, as I said in my testimony we are focused to holding elections on April 30th. This will be the third full term election for a 4-year government, first one December 2005 and then 2010 and then this year.

As you may know, the head of the main Sunni coalition, Osama al-Nujaifi, was in the United States 2 weeks ago. He had meetings with the President and the Vice President. He met the Secretary of State at his home.

So we are very focused on making sure that the elections happen, that they produce a genuine and credible result and that they allow a government to reform that reflects the make-up of Iraqi society with all represented.

In Fallujah, as I described in my testimony the plan is to have the tribes out in front but with the army in support because this is—they face—ISIL is an army. They have heavy weapons. They have 50-caliber sniper rifles. They are very well trained and very well fortified.

So we have to have the Sunnis, tribal local people out in front but they will require security support. And General Austin was in Iraq last week for direct talks with Iraqi military commanders. We are advising the commanders as best we can, building on the lessons that we learned in these areas for tactical and strategic patience, for planning and to make sure that civilian casualties are minimized.

Ms. ROS-LEHTINEN. Thank you so much.

I know how hard you have been working, and to paraphrase Ambassador Crocker everything about Iraq is hard all the time. So please keep making progress.

Thank you, sir.

Chairman ROYCE. Mr. Sherman of California. Thank you.

Mr. SHERMAN. There was bipartisan support for leaving a residual force in Iraq. That required a status of forces agreement with the Maliki government, and the status of forces agreement would have had to have included immunity for our soldiers so that they would not be subject to Iraqi courts.

We ask our soldiers, Marines, airmen, et cetera, to take many risks. One of them we don't ask them to take is the idea that their actions would be held up to judgment in a court in Iraq or a court in Afghanistan, for that matter.

We didn't get a status of forces agreement. One theory is the administration blew the negotiations. The other view is the Maliki government was in place when this administration got there. Maliki didn't have to give immunity to our troops and chose not to.

We've seen that these immunity agreements are difficult for a host country to provide. Karzai isn't providing them and there are several elements of Iranian history going back 70 or 80 years where the Shah was held up to great ridicule for providing such immunity agreements.

Did we fail to get a status of forces agreement because we blew the negotiations or, given the political reality starting with Maliki, was there simply no way to get the immunity?

Mr. MCGURK. First, keying on the history is really important here. The history of immunity agreements, particularly in this region, is really what colors the entire debate.

The negotiation in 2007 and 2008 took almost 18 months, and while we got those two agreements passed, the security agreement which allowed our forces to stay for 3 more years with immunities and a permanent strategic framework agreement they barely passed.

They passed on the last possible day and almost by the skin of their teeth, and I was working on that issue with Ambassador Crocker for almost 18 months.

Mr. SHERMAN. This is passing the Iraqi Parliament?

Mr. MCGURK. Yes, the Iraqi Parliament. Our legal requirements in 2011 were that another follow-on agreement would have to go through the Iraqi Parliament.

It was the assessment of the Iraqi political leaders and also of our leadership that it was unlikely to pass and therefore the decision was made that our troops leave by the end of 2011.

But we still have a permanent strategic framework agreement. That agreement has passed the Iraqi Parliament. It was ratified in 2008 and it provides us a strong basis for providing security assistance to the Iraqis.

It does not provide us a basis for having boots on the ground and a training presence. But we do train Iraqi special forces under our Office of Security Cooperation through the Embassy and we're also in discussions with regional partners for having a training presence.

Mr. SHERMAN. Okay. I want to move on to another question.

Has there been discussion of the U.S. Air Force or other air force—naval air forces bombing these al-Qaeda camps rather than us providing huge amounts of weaponry to Maliki so that he can try to do it himself? And has there been discussion of U.S. Air Force's preventing overflights by the Iranians since the Iraqis say they can't control their own airspace?

Mr. MCGURK. No, there's not been discussion of a direct U.S. role in controlling Iraqi airspace or in targeting the camps. We're very focused on increasing the Iraqi capacity to be able to target camps and they've proven effective in recent months.

Mr. SHERMAN. I would point out that if only we were bombing al-Qaeda camps before—the years before 9/11 we may have had a very different history.

We see the residents of Camp Ashraf, 52 of them killed last September—in December, another four killed. The Secretary of State has appointed a special advisor on MEK resettlement.

What is the status of protecting these folks while they're there and insisting that Iraq meet its legal obligations to do so and of finding homes outside the region for some of the residents?

Mr. MCGURK. Let me make a couple points. When I was here in November, I explained that there is a cell, we believe, trained by Iran and it is dedicated to attacking the MEK at Camp Liberty.

We had cells trained by Iran dedicated to attacking us when we had a military presence in Iraq. We did everything we could to root those cells out and it was very difficult. We were never able to do so.

So the only place that these people will be safe is outside of Iraq and that's why we are focused, as you said. Jonathan Weiner has been appointed to work this issue full time as a senior advisor for MEK resettlement to find a safe secure relocation for the residents of Camp Liberty.

But while they're at Camp Liberty, the governor of Iraq has an obligation to do everything it can to keep them safe and that means T-walls and that means protection and that is something we raise constantly to make sure that they are getting as much protection as possible.

You also mentioned some other notable developments and there's finally some real international tension to this urgent humanitarian crisis. First, there is a U.N.-created resettlement fund.

We have notified Congress for $1 million to put into that resettlement fund. When I was in Iraq last week on Tuesday, the Iraqi cabinet authorized $500,000 to be allocated to that resettlement fund.

The United Nations has also appointed Jane Holl Lute full time basis to focus on MEK resettlement. So we are getting some progress and I look forward to working with you and the committee and the Congress to try to move this forward in the coming weeks.

Chairman ROYCE. We go now to Mr. Chris Smith of New Jersey.

Mr. SMITH. Thank you very much, Mr. Chairman, and Secretary McGurk, thank you for your service and thank you for being here today. Just a few questions.

You mentioned that on January 1st and reminded us 70 to 100 trucks entered Fallujah and Ramadi. Was that a tactical surprise on the part of the ISIL or did we have intelligence that suggested they were mustering and that they were about to move or did the Iraqis have that intelligence, and if we did what was done with that?

Secondly, you talked about how the suicide bombers in a turn of twisted logic has become the most precious resource and, ominously, you point out that in November 2012 there were three suicide bombings and that has gone up to 50.

What is the glide scope on that? Is that continually expanding as—do we expect it to be 100 by November of next year or has that ebbed? If you could speak to that issue.

Third, you point out that ISIS has set their sights on Baghdad in the south. You quote Abu Bakr al-Baghdadi on January 21st. How seriously is that threat to Baghdad?

Fourth, if you could, you point out the ISIL execution of Iraqi soldiers, that the Maliki soldiers did not take the bait—the army. But is that something that's ongoing? Are they executing police? Are they holding prisoners in center city Fallujah or the central part of it, I should say, of Fallujah?

And then when it comes to the issue of Christians, the USCIRF report—the Commission of Religious Freedom points out that the Iraqi Government continues to tolerate systematic, ongoing and egregious religious freedom violations and that is against a number of the smaller sects, many of them going back 2,000 years including the Chaldo-Assyrians.

What is happening? What kind of pressure are we trying to put on that government to get them to mitigate and hopefully completely end their repression of Christians in Iraq?

And finally, you talked about the low boil type of insurgency that this represents. Are we looking at the possibility of another Syria in Iraq?

Mr. McGURK. Thank you, Congressman. Let me try to address these issues, first, in terms of the entry into Fallujah and Ramadi.

We started to see, as the Iraqis started to hit some of the encampments, kind of moving around of the ISIL forces and trying to relocate. Their entre en masse on New Year's Day was a surprise.

Again, I think it was a tactical mistake on ISIL's part. This isn't going to turn overnight but there has been a response. As I described in my testimony, in Ramadi the response developed fairly rapidly to actually expel them from the streets. In Fallujah, it's going to be far harder.

But one thing that—the Sunnis in Anbar Province they may not like the government. They may not even trust the army. But they really don't like these foreign jihadist fighters.

So we're trying to kind of gather common cause against them. In terms of the suicide bombers, the average now is about 30 to 40 a week. I don't think this will be an exponential rise. I'm hoping that the—kind of 50 might be, you know, a cap.

We saw this problem and phenomenon in the past and what we did in 2006 and 2008 was a very concerted regional wide effort—how do you get these people with a one-way ticket—then they're flying into Damascus—military-age males with a one-way to Damascus off the airplanes, and we were fairly effective actually at draining the flow, and one thing that drained the flow was increasing security in western Iraq. So we're going to try to recreate that strategy throughout the region.

ISIL's strategy to attack the south—they are trying to attack the south. I would not be surprised if they're on the same play book from 2006. You may remember that after the election in December 2005 it was in late February that al-Qaeda in Iraq then attacked the Samarra mosque, which really kind of led to the sectarian violence which you saw for the next 2 years.

I think they are going to try to attack very high profile targets in the south, particularly religiously symbolic targets. I hope and I don't think they will be successful. I think the Iraqis have those areas pretty well protected. But it's definitely part of their strategy.

In terms of Fallujah, yes, we do believe that Iraqi soldiers are being held in Fallujah and, as I said, these extremists are fighters. They're trying to goad the army into a direct urban confrontation.

So far, despite some rhetoric you might see about storming Fallujah, that is not the strategy that is underway. But the government does have responsibility working with the local people to secure Fallujah and I think there will be—there will be fighting, particularly in the outskirts and then later in the central city.

But we're going to try to make sure it is as contained as possible. And on Christians, a very good question. We're very focused on the plight of Christians in Iraq but also throughout the region.

When Prime Minister Maliki was here he acknowledged in his public remarks the importance of taking care of the Christian community. In October, he met with Patriarch Sako, the head of the Chaldean Church.

When I am in Iraq I try to meet with Christian leaders. I met with Archbishop Warda in Erbil a couple months ago and tried to focus on some of their land disputes they're having there. The Iraqi cabinet recently passed a resolution to talk about carving out a Christian province to allow them some autonomy and security.

Again, this is something that we continue to develop. I'm going to be meeting with an Iraqi Christian leader tomorrow in my office. So we're very focused on it but it's an extremely, extremely difficult issue. Christians are threatened by these extremists as are Sunnis and everybody—Sunni, Shi'a, everybody.

Chairman ROYCE. Thank you.

Mr. Sires of New Jersey.

Mr. SIRES. Thank you, Mr. Chairman, and thank you for being here.

You know, the ties between Iraq and Iran seems to be getting closer. They signed a defense—have a defense treaty that supposedly they put together.

I am concerned that maybe the safety of people at Camp Liberty the Iraqis are not making the effort that they really need to secure these people. If I'm making an arms contract with—a treaty with Iran, why would I be so intent on the safety of these people?

Just in December they keep firing rockets into this—into this camp. So how sure are you that they're making the best possible effort to bring security to this camp?

Mr. McGURK. Congressman, the issue remains extremely, extremely difficult. There was a rocket attack in the camp earlier this month and I would just remind you there was a rocket attack at Camp Cropper, which is right near Camp Liberty which used to house our soldiers, and we took casualties as late as summer of 2011, and that's when we had about 70,000 troops in the country trying to stop this kind of activity.

It's very difficult to deter and to root out a well-trained team with rockets and that is why we're trying to move as much protection into the camp as possible. That's why I went to the camp myself—to see it, to meet with the residents and to try to assess the security and protection. It remains a very difficult issue.

I'll be honest. The MEK doesn't like the Iraqi Government. The Iraqi Government doesn't like the MEK, and it's a very dynamic issue and all we got to do is stay on the MEK to do everything they can to cooperate, to move the residents to a safe and secure location and stay on the government.

Every time I meet with the leaders of the government I mention this issue. Despite all the other issues they're dealing with, I mention it every single time and as I said, I just received a report this morning that T-walls are moving back into the camp and we're going to make sure that they continue to move back in the camp tomorrow, the next day and the day after.

Mr. SIRES. How concerned are you about the treaty between Iraq and Iran, this defense treaty, the arms going into Iraq?

Mr. McGURK. The Iraqis have been pretty careful to draw a line in terms of security cooperation with Iran and so far they've kept that line fairly firm. So I've seen reports like that but I would not take it too seriously.

Iraq has made—the Iraqis have made clear they want a long-term institutional relationship with the United States and they want the United States to be the backbone of their military, and that's why they want platforms like an Apache helicopter system.

When we sell a country an Apache helicopter we're not just giving them an attack helicopter. We're actually—we're buying a 30-year relationship in terms of training pilots, logistics, maintenance and that's why we feel it's so important.

The F–16 program is the same. We want Iraq to have a long-term institutional relationship military to military with the United States. In General Austin's visit to Iraq last week he, of course, knows the Iraqi commanders. They've led together in the streets and the fields of Baghdad and the outskirts and all throughout Iraq and they have very deep, deep relationships.

And I was in those meetings and you cannot get a deeper relationship than people who have fought side by side, and that is something that we are going to continue to develop. You know, Maliki is the Prime Minister now. He might be the Prime Minister after the coming elections. He might not be.

What we're focused on is building an institutional relationship with the Iraqi Government and the institutions—the military, the Parliament, something that's going to last for many, many years.

Mr. SIRES. And the sale of Russian arms to Iraq, are you concerned about that at all—$4 billion, whatever it was?

Mr. McGURK. Yes. I don't want Iraqis buying Russian hardware and, you know, but I have to be honest. Given the security situation there's a lot of strategic competitors in Baghdad showing up, knocking on the same doors we're knocking on and saying hey, we're here to sell you an attack helicopter, just write a check.

We have a system through our foreign military sales system, which is a good system, it makes sure that the stuff arrives with a long-term institutional relationship, as I discussed. But it's slow and cumbersome.

Earlier this month, I was in Saudi Arabia, Bahrain and other countries and there was a lot of, you know, complaints about our foreign military sales system is too slow. We hear the same thing from the Iraqis.

But I want Iraq to buy U.S. equipment because that buys a long-term strategic relationship. So yes, you know, it's unfortunate that they bought the MI–35s from the Russians but on the other hand, you know, they kept telling us they were going to do it if we couldn't get them the Apaches fast enough.

Mr. SIRES. And there's no consideration to giving them drones, right? Selling drones to the Iraqis?

Mr. McGURK. Well, we are selling them unmanned UAVs. Not armed drones but we're selling them——

Mr. SIRES. I meant armed.

Mr. McGURK. Yes. No, armed drones is not under consideration.

Mr. SIRES. Okay. Thank you.

Ms. ROS-LEHTINEN. Thank you.

We now turn to Mr. Rohrabacher for his questions.

Mr. ROHRABACHER. Thank you very much, and we're all impressed with your knowledge level you're able to do this and from your memory and we're impressed by that. I'm impressed by that. But that doesn't mean that I agree with your assessment.

Let me just say that the idea that—we're talking about Camp Ashraf. It seems that fundamentally you're suggesting that our approach to try to stop the massacre—the ongoing massacre of the people at Camp Liberty that we basically have to go to the Maliki government and ask them and the problem is they're not providing enough security.

The Maliki government is responsible for these deaths. I don't understand. The military, the Iraqi military, invaded Camp Ashraf and murdered people. These are the people under Maliki's command did that.

They recently went into—the 50 that were so left at Camp Ashraf, tied their hands behind their back and shot them in the back of the head and it was Maliki's own military we know who did that.

We know that the Camp Ashraf and these people were attacked numerous times by the Iraqi military. This isn't whether Maliki and his people are not protecting the MEK. This is a crime against humanity. These are unarmed refugees in which Maliki's own troops are murdering.

We're not talking about, you know, rockets that we don't know where they come from. We're talking about actual—by the way, I would suggest that they probably know about those rockets as well.

Maliki—let's make it very clear. As far as I'm concerned and as far as many people in Washington are concerned, Maliki is an accomplice to the murders that are going on, and as an accomplice we should not be treating him, begging him, to have a residual force of U.S. troops in order to help his regime.

I don't understand why the United States feels like—we feel compelled to be part of all of this. Why do we feel compelled that we have to go in and be in the middle of a fight between people who are murdering each other? Thirty to 40 suicide bombers a month? Thousands of people are losing their lives to this insanity.

Why should the United States, tell me—this is my question—why does the United States feel that we need to become part of this insanity and does that not instead turn both of the parties against us?

Mr. McGurk. Congressman, the suicide bomber phenomenon, it is complete insanity. I agree with you.

When you look at Iraq and you look at the region and you define our interests, and I don't go with any leader and beg for anything but we protect and advance U.S. interests as we define them, and in Iraq, whether you like it or not, oil, al-Qaeda, Iran, vital U.S. interests are at stake in Iraq. So we need to do what we can without putting U.S. personnel——

Mr. Rohrabacher. Why shouldn't we let them kill each other? Let them kill each other. I'm sorry. If it means that we're going to spend our treasure and more of our blood—we've already spent thousands of lives of American soldiers.

We've done enough, and I'm so happy that you now can report to us that your negotiations to provide a residual American military force in Iraq was not successful because I'm very happy that we don't have a bunch of American troops in the middle of that mess.

And if we're not even—we are not even capable of letting Maliki know that we're holding him responsible for the murders in his own ranks, for the people—for the military that he commands to go into Camp Ashraf and Camp Liberty and murder unarmed refugees.

This is a no-win situation for us. Both sides seem to be evil—both sides or all the sides. One last question. I've got 30 seconds.

Who is financing? You talked about 100 trucks and all of this equipment costs money. Bullets even cost money. AK–47s cost money. Rockets cost money. Who is paying for all of that, the mayhem on both sides of this fight?

Mr. MCGURK. Congressman, I defer to my intelligence colleagues for the specific funding. But we believe it's the whole source of funding but private funding from throughout the region funding the global jihadist movement which is now really based in Syria and the region.

Mr. ROHRABACHER. Is that the Saudis?

Mr. MCGURK. Again, I would have to defer to my intelligence colleagues for that sort of information. But a lot of it is private—you know, private funding.

Mr. ROHRABACHER. Private funds. Thank you very much.

Chairman ROYCE. Mr. McGurk, while you're on the subject—while we're on the subject, did you want to share any details in terms of the attack on Camp Ashraf and, in your judgment, who you believe was involved in that, since that was the question at hand?

Mr. MCGURK. Thank you, Mr. Chairman.

I think the last time I was here I discussed what we know. We believe it was a militia. We believe the militia was trained by Iran and that's really the primary responsibility, and we have—since that very horrific attack we worked to get the survivors out of Camp Ashraf, which is about, you know, 40 miles from the Iranian border, and onto Camp Liberty.

Camp Liberty is not safe but it's safer. We have the U.N. in the camp every day monitoring the camp and, again, when I go to try to go to the camp and meet with the survivors and the residents there. So we're doing——

Chairman ROYCE. And you're making efforts right now to relocate the survivors?

Mr. MCGURK. Absolutely. Yes.

Chairman ROYCE. Okay. We're going to go now to Mr. Gerry Connolly from Virginia.

Mr. CONNOLLY. Thank you, Mr. Chairman, and welcome, Mr. McGurk.

Couple of questions first. The authorization for the use of military force, the administration has indicated it would not oppose the repeal of that. Is the issue the timing with respect to, say, pending elections in Iraq? Might it disrupt things you're doing in Iraq if we were to do that now?

Mr. MCGURK. Congressman, I don't think there's much focus on that in Iraq so I don't think it would make much of a difference——

Mr. CONNOLLY. Okay.

Mr. MCGURK [continuing]. In terms of from the Iraqi perspective.

Mr. CONNOLLY. That's good to know. Okay.

Elections in April still on schedule?

Mr. MCGURK. We—our team at the Embassy is talking every day to the United Nations assistant mission in Iraq and the Iraqi High Electoral Commission, which are planning elections, and the information I have received most recently is that elections do remain on track.

We have tens of thousands of displaced families from Anbar Province. We have been assured by those planning the elections that displaced people will still be able to vote and the vote will count as if they were in their home province.

So we are still confident the election will be held on April 30th and our consistent position and very firm position is that those elections have to be held on April 30th. There should not be a delay.

Mr. CONNOLLY. What a novel thought, allowing people to vote remotely—a thought here for the United States.

But Fallujah—help us understand what happened. I mean, the United States has been involved now for 12 years. Billions and billions of dollars—we've reconstituted the Iraqi military. We have trained, you know, law enforcement forces.

We spent our military's blood and treasure to gain a foothold, to gain Fallujah, and, you know, al-Qaeda's success or organization manages to occupy it. And if I understood your testimony correctly, we're now once again relying on tribal support to essentially dislodge the occupying forces in Fallujah.

How in the world—isn't that an indictment of the investments we've made in the Iraqi military and its inability to hold its own territory secure?

Mr. McGURK. The Iraqi military would have the numbers and the equipment to go into Fallujah tomorrow and clean out the streets. We believe that were they to do an assault like that that it would actually exacerbate the problem. So——

Mr. CONNOLLY. I guess—excuse me 1 second, Mr. McGurk.

I don't mean—but before you get there, but how did it happen in the first place? How is it that the Iraqi Government was not able to secure something as symbolically important if not really important as Fallujah?

Mr. McGURK. As I tried to explain in my testimony, there was a series of events throughout 2013 including a protest movement which kind of added to the political instability in the region, and in Fallujah in particular it is an area, as we know, any outsiders coming into Fallujah are resisted and that includes the Iraqi army, it included us and it includes, we hope now, these al-Qaeda extremists.

You know, all I can say is we are where we are right now and we're helping the Iraqis develop a plan—they're developing a plan, one that will lead—I say tribal fighters. What we really mean is that the local people, local population who know the streets, who are able to actually identify the foreign elements and push them out.

But right now in Fallujah, it's a mix of al-Qaeda, former insurgent groups and former Ba'athist networks who are in control of the streets there. It has always been a very difficult place and so it's just a very difficult territory to operate in.

Mr. CONNOLLY. The tribal support we're relying on or cooperating with what is their attitude toward the Maliki government? I mean, because doesn't some of that support and cooperation, isn't some of that a function of how they view the central government?

Mr. MCGURK. Yes. Certainly, there's tremendous mistrust in the area of Fallujah toward the central government. There's no question about that.

Mr. CONNOLLY. And does that impede our ability to try to dislodge the occupation forces in Fallujah?

Mr. MCGURK. It does. It makes it—it makes it harder. As I said, some tribes are actually working with the extremists. Some are now working to oust them and many others are on the fence, and that's why it's incumbent upon the central government through resources and through dialogue and communication to mobilize the population against them.

And when we worked with the Awakening we did three things. We trusted them, we funded them but also significantly we protected them. They thought they were going to win.

Sheikh Abdul Sattar, who was the head of the Awakening in the early days, we parked two M–1 tanks in front of his villa and he was still killed by a suicide bomber.

So, you know, this is a very tough area and these are tough folks. But the tribal leaders need to know that they're going to be supported and they believe they're going to win, and that's why Maliki's commitment most recently to give tribal fighters all the benefits of an Iraqi soldier and to incorporate those fighters into the security structures of the state, meaning they'll have a livelihood going forward to protect their people, is a very significant commitment.

It's one that's never been made before and we now need to make sure that we hold the government to it and follow through.

Mr. CONNOLLY. Thank you. Thank you, Mr. Chairman.

Chairman ROYCE. Judge Ted Poe from Texas.

Mr. POE. Thank you, Mr. Chairman.

I want to talk about what you probably thought I would talk about today is the MEK. The last time you were here and you testified before my subcommittee and the chairwoman, Ileana Ros-Lehtinen's, subcommittee I made the statement that there would probably be more attacks on Camp Liberty and, unfortunately, I was correct. Camp Liberty was attacked again—four people killed, seven injured. One young man lost both of his legs.

Since 2009, there have been seven attacks on Camp Liberty or Camp Ashraf. During that time, 19 times members of the State Department have testified. Most of those or many of those were about Camp Liberty in addition to other things.

In all those attacks, to my knowledge as of today, not one person has been captured or charged with any of those killings—not one, and they're still on the loose.

As I alluded to in my testimony, I personally believe that the Maliki government is in cahoots with the Iranian Government to let Camp Liberty, Camp Ashraf be subject to attacks. These last attacks, from my understanding, were rockets came in that were three meters long, 40 of them.

It seems impossible to me that a rogue Iranian militia could sneak those by anybody and then fire them over a period of time and cause this chaos and murder, and I bring this up for several reasons.

One, it hadn't been resolved. But this has become very personal to people who live in my district. I represent people who are Iranian-Americans. They know these people that are being killed. They are family. They are friends. And they come and they visit and they tell us it's happened again, Judge Poe, with tears in their eyes.

So it's become personal. Many of those people are sitting behind you and they come up here wanting help. That's all they want. The United States has, you know, said that we promised to help them.

We've just—we no longer recognize them as a foreign terrorist organization. They just want their loved ones safe, safe first from the constant attacks by the—well, I believe the Iraqi and the Iranians working together, but long term they want to leave. They want to be in a safe country.

Now, when you visited, and I commend you for going to visit the camp, did you see these—what looked like graves but they are really—what these are used for the people at Camp Liberty are in such fear of their lives they no longer stay in these trailer houses here.

They have dug themselves what looks like a grave to hide in when the attacks come from the rockets and they dig these and they put sandbags around them and then they're ready for the next attack.

They jump in these things. Some of them sleep in these things at night, even in the rain, to try to be safe—literally digging their own graves.

This is—it seems to me this is a fairly tragic situation when people live like this in fear of where they are, whether it's the Iraqis, whether it's the Iranians or both. Were you able—did you see any of this when you were there, these—what they use as now foxholes to hide in from the rockets?

Mr. MCGURK. I didn't see that particular lane but I saw some of the bunkers in the—at the camp.

Mr. POE. Well, I'm sure you'll see it on your next visit. But, now, this is what they have resorted to for their own safety. I think that is an international human rights concern. It should be.

The T-walls—you mentioned T-walls are coming. My understanding they hadn't gotten any T-walls today. Seventeen thousand of them were removed in a short period of time. Now they're wanting to put them back in slowly. It's a safety hazard.

They just want these T-walls to be safe. They ought to move them in now. The other concern that I wanted to mention is the resettlement issue. They want to leave Iraq. We want them to leave. The Iraqis want them to leave.

The Iranians want them to—I'm not so sure what the Iranians want. But the West constantly says because the United States has not taken any of these people we're not going to take them either. When the U.S. starts leading by example rather than just talking about removing these people then maybe we'll take them as well.

Why haven't these folks been sent to other countries? Why haven't we taken some of them or all of them? That's my first question. And the second question is when you visited with the survivors of the Ashraf Camp attack, did they tell you who they believed was responsible for attacking them and killing their families and their friends? Those are the two questions I have.

Mr. McGurk. Let me, first, say in terms of accountability, a Shi'a militia leader who took responsibility for the attacks openly and was on Iraqi television giving interviews, taking responsibility for attacking the camp. We thought it was ridiculous that this guy was walking the streets inciting people to attack the camp.

He was arrested by Iraqi security forces and is detained and is being investigated. So that is something that happened in the last month. I agree with you that this is an international human rights concern.

That is why, as I mentioned in my response earlier, I find it encouraging that there is now United Nations focus with the resettlement fund, a full time person at the United Nations to focus on this issue.

And as you also correctly point out, very few countries around the world, despite the international human rights concern, have agreed to take the residents into their territory—Albania, Germany, a total of about 350. So we still have almost 2,900 people at the camp.

This is an international human rights concern and it has to be treated with the utmost urgency. As you know, we are considering options to relocate and integrate camp residents in the United States, in close coordination with the White House Department of Homeland Security and other relevant agencies, and any eligible residents would have to be fully vetted, of course, under our standards by the Department of Homeland Security. That is something that we are actively, actively, actively considering, I can assure you.

But we also, and I would encourage those who care about the residents as do we to lobby other capitals around the world, given that this is an international human rights concern, to take residents into their territory because so long as they are in Iraq they will not be safe.

And you're right, four residents of the camp lost their lives, tragically, this month. Nine hundred Iraqis also lost their lives this month.

Iraq is a very violent place and particularly the residents at Camp Liberty will not be safe until they leave and that is why we have a full time person working on it.

We encourage the U.N. and they have now appointed a full time person to work on the problem and we have a U.N. resettlement fund to encourage other countries to take the residents in, and until they're out of Iraq they won't be safe.

Chairman Royce. And now we go to Mr. Ted Deutch of Florida. Thank you.

Mr. Deutch. Thank you, Mr. Chairman.

Mr. McGurk, thanks for being here. Thanks for your thoughtful testimony.

Last year, we wrote a letter to the Prime Minister about the flight—the overflights of Iranian aircraft. There are reports that the number of overflights from Iran has increased, that these are flights that Iran sends to arm Hezbollah to expand their influence in Syria to defend the Assad regime even as it slaughters—continues to slaughter its own people.

How do you characterize Prime Minister Maliki's relationship with Iran?

Mr. MCGURK. Let me say a couple words about Iran's nefarious role in Iraq.

Just like al-Qaeda has exploited the grievances of the Sunni community, Iran is exploiting the fears and apprehensions of the Shi'a community as they are attacked by these al-Qaeda extremists.

So it's a vicious cycle that Iran very much takes advantage of in their most extreme elements of that regime and the Quds Force.

Maliki, and we discuss this with him all the time, you know, tries to balance all these many pressures that come at Baghdad from the region and from internal debates.

He is under great pressure from his constituency, particularly among the Shi'a who continue to get attacked by these extremist groups. But so far we have seen the Iraqi Government resist the Iranian efforts to have a direct security role in Iraq.

Iran still, we believe, controls certain militia groups in Iraq, although their activities are not nearly to the level that they were 4 or 5 years ago.

Mr. DEUTCH. So they've resisted Iran's efforts to play a more significant role in Iraq but they've resisted the efforts of many of us here to convince them to play a more significant role in stopping these overflights. Why don't they do it?

Mr. MCGURK. Again, the overflights are something that—all I can say is we continue to raise the overflight issue. We believe some of this material, a lot of it, is coming on civilian flights.

We do have certain agreements with the Iraqis, which we look forward to testing as soon as we have intelligence we're able to share with them in terms of actually catching a flight in the act. But we've not been able to test that yet. So——

Mr. DEUTCH. I'm sorry. Say that again. You've—explain that.

Mr. MCGURK. Well, we have agreements with Iraq. It's very hard to get a precise intelligence picture in terms of what's coming on a flight and when. It's just very difficult.

But when we do—and we've worked with countries around the region in similar circumstances—when we do we hope to be able to work with the Iraqis to be able to make sure that we're able to stop or deter that flight.

Mr. DEUTCH. Right. Here's what I'm—here's what I'm trying to get at. It is difficult to identify what's on the planes. I understand that.

Much of the frustration that I have on this issue is frustration generally with what's happening in Syria and the ongoing assertion by so many that it's hard.

So much about Syria is hard, and it's difficult even as there are now more than 130,000 Syrians who have been slaughtered. So this is one very small area where it is difficult.

Yet, do you believe that the Maliki government, that the Prime Minister discounts the suggestion that there are planes flying from Iran full of weapons that are flying over Iraq with those weapons to be delivered to Hezbollah, used to prop up Assad's regime and to kill the Syrian people?

Mr. MCGURK. Do I believe he believes that and knows it's actually happening?

Mr. DEUTCH. Mm-hmm. Right.

Mr. McGURK. I think we've given him enough information to provide a reasonable assurance.

Mr. DEUTCH. Then when do we start—how do we test these? You said we need to start testing some of this. When are we going to start testing? How do we do that?

How do we—this is—again, this is one very discrete and this—I'm just bringing in everything else that goes into Syria at the moment, which this committee had focused on extensively and will continue to focus on extensively.

But with this one very discrete area, one very discrete point—that is, weapons from Iran to Hezbollah that fly over Iraq—it's one very discrete area where perhaps we can have some—play some greater role in making it even slightly more difficult for Hezbollah to help Assad as he murders his own people, slightly more difficult if our ally in Iraq plays a more constructive role.

So how do we test that? How do we get—how do we make that happen?

Mr. McGURK. First, I would be happy to come discuss in a different setting specifically some of the issues related to this topic.

But I can just put you in the picture. When we have these conversations with Iraqi officials and leaders, as soon as you mention Syria what they talk about in Syria is the threat that is coming from Syria into Iraq and it's a very real threat, and that is, like, their primary threat perception coming from Syria.

We explain that the reason the terrorist groups are entrenching in Syria is partially due to Assad who, as the Secretary said, is a terror magnet, and so long as the Assad regime is able to be strengthened this vicious cycle is going to go on. The Iraqis have signed up to Geneva 1 communique.

They've done some things consistent with our efforts to try to put pressure on Assad, and on the overflight issue all I can say I've been in Iraq twice this month and has raised this issue specifically to get inspections increased again, and the next time I'm here I hope to report some progress.

Mr. DEUTCH. Thank you very much, Mr. McGurk. Yield back.

Chairman ROYCE. Mr. Deutch. We go now to Mr. George Holding of North Carolina.

Mr. HOLDING. Thank you, Mr. Chairman.

Mr. McGurk, I appreciate your level of knowledge and facility with the facts and your ability to communicate them.

In numerous answers you detailed the support that Iran is giving to militias in Iraq and to al-Qaeda-related and successor al-Qaeda groups in Iraq who are propagating this violence and undoing, I think, a lot of the good work that we were able to do in Iraq.

In addition to that, where the Maliki government may be able to disavow it and say that, you know, we're not supportive of what Iran is doing in Iraq on that level, there are other areas which are in contravention of the sanctions that we've placed on Iran such as in the energy area—the energy sector.

You know, it's come to light that in the Basra Province, you know, Iran and Iraq are negotiating the building of a pipeline to supply gas into two new power plants there, this all in contravention, you know, of the sanctions.

Are we putting Iraq on notice that this is in contravention to the sanctions and detrimental to what we perceive as our interest?

Mr. MCGURK. A very good question and this is also an ongoing topic of conversation. They share a 3,000-kilometer border so there is trade. There's cultural ties. It's impossible to stop everything.

The Iraqis have been very conscious of trying to enforce—make sure that they are working consistent with our sanctions. In fact, they have not paid Iran for arrears that they're owed for certain electricity payments because they believe that it might be sanctionable even though the banks in which they would pay are not sanctionable banks.

So the Iraqis have tried to even go an extra mile in terms of a sanctionable—making sure that they are staying and keeping with our——

Mr. HOLDING. And with regard to financial institutions, I mean, there's a great deal of evidence that, you know, the nature of the relationship between Iraqi financial institutions and Iranian financial institutions goes way beyond what would be permitted, you know, under the sanctions.

Mr. MCGURK. I have to—maybe I could follow up with you specifically on this because it's a very detailed topic. But Iraqi banks have cut off many transactions with Iranian banks simply due to reputational risk.

Iraq has also increased its oil output while Iran has asked them not to do that because we've taken 1 million barrels of Iranian oil off the market.

So, again, this is constant. But the pipeline you mentioned is concerning. If that pipeline goes forward that could indeed fall afoul of our sanctions.

Mr. HOLDING. You know, considering the extreme, you know, detriment to our interests from this Iranian support of militant groups in Iraq, is there any part of the nuclear deal that the administration is currently negotiating that would address these issues to, you know, put it as a condition? You know, Iran you've got to stop doing this.

Mr. MCGURK. Congressman, the nuclear negotiation is focused solely on the nuclear proliferation issues but that does not mean that we are not also focused on——

Mr. HOLDING. So we're not using any leverage or any of our capital in lifting the sanctions for the nuclear enrichment part of it to try to solve some of the other problems we're having in Iraq with Iran?

Mr. MCGURK. Given the existential threat that a nuclear-armed Iran would pose to our interests in the region, we focused the nuclear negotiations specifically on the nuclear issue to try to get at that.

Mr. HOLDING. As far as Iranian support of Hezbollah which, as you say, pointed out that you've given Maliki clear, clear evidence of, you know, what's going on as far as the overflights go and the supply of Hezbollah with Iranian weapons, is there any part in the nuclear negotiations that we're doing now with Iran which would address Iranian support of Hezbollah fighters in Syria?

Mr. McGURK. Again, the nuclear negotiations are focussed on the nuclear proliferation issues specifically but that does not mean we don't deal with the other issues on parallel and separate tracks.

Mr. HOLDING. But, again, we're not using any of the leverage that we have in the nuclear negotiations to try to address the situation we have with Hezbollah and Syria?

Mr. McGURK. We're not discussing those through the nuclear channel, no.

Mr. HOLDING. Okay. Thank you.

Mr. Chairman, I yield back.

Mr. KINZINGER. The gentleman yields back. Chair now recognizes Mr. Cicilline for 5 minutes.

Mr. CICILLINE. Thank you, Mr. Chairman. Thank you, Mr. McGurk, for being here and for your insightful testimony this morning.

As you can imagine, events in Iraq are particularly difficult to hear about in light of the heroic sacrifice of American heroes and the billions and billions of dollars of taxpayer money expended in this region of the world and you acknowledge that in your written testimony, and I thank you for that.

I'd ask you to first speak a little bit to the difference of events in Ramadi and Fallujah. It seems as if the turnaround in Ramadi was quick and fairly effective and, obviously, that is not the case in Fallujah.

Would you speak a little bit about why that is, the extent of the coordination between the tribal fighters and the Iraqi Government and resource allocations between these two cities and any other factors which are contributing to either different outcomes or different strategies?

Mr. McGURK. I think Fallujah has always just been the most hardened—the most hardened part of the insurgency when we were fighting it and it's just—it's a different environment.

If you look at the protest movement over 2013, the protests in Ramadi remained generally of a moderate tone focussed on the legitimate grievances of the community. The protests in Fallujah, which also took place every Friday, were far more militant, far more extremist.

So it's just a different environment, just like many, you know, cities in different countries have different cultures and different attitudes.

Mr. CICILLINE. And if I could just follow up on Congressman Deutch's question, I think you said that most of the foreign fighters were Syrian. Is that right?

Mr. McGURK. No, foreign fighters who come in to Syria. So from the greater region and global jihadist-minded people who come in to Syria to fight jihad and are——

Mr. CICILLINE. Are then coming into Iraq.

Mr. McGURK [continuing]. Put into a suicide bomb track.

Mr. CICILLINE. And so would you speak a little more about what the relationship is between the Maliki government and President Maliki in particular and President Assad? And so do they understand that by allowing these flyovers and potentially strengthening or prolonging the Assad regime they actually are undermining their ability to take back their own country from these same extremists.

I mean, do they make that connection? What is the relationship between the Maliki administration—Maliki regime and the Assad regime?

Mr. McGurk. Maliki and the top leaders of the Iraqi Government, there's no love lost with Bashar al-Assad. If you look at 2009, Maliki was calling for Assad to be brought to a criminal court at the time based upon some bombings which happened in August 2009 that the Iraqi Government blamed on the Syrian regime. Again, they've signed on to the Geneve communique which prefaces that there will be a transition without Bashar al-Assad.

I'll be perfectly candid. When we explained to them that Bashar al-Assad remaining in power is a magnet for jihadis and terrorists who are coming into Iraq that is a train of logic that many Iraqi officials don't agree with, frankly. They believe that if Assad left that the regime would collapse and make the problem worse.

So this is a constant—you know, just seeing the same picture we do they don't see it but we believe very strongly, as the Secretary has said a number of times, and the President that Bashar al-Assad in power is a magnet for these foreign fighters coming into Syria to fight a jihad.

And until he is removed from power, we're going to continue to be in this very vicious cycle which is going to have pernicious effects on all of Syria's neighbors—Iraq, Lebanon and Jordan, in particular.

Mr. Cicilline. But, I mean, what other tools do we have at our disposal to persuade the Maliki government that that is the case? Because otherwise we're going to be left in a position where they're going to continue to implicitly or explicitly support the Assad regime in the context of flyovers or other efforts.

Mr. McGurk. I think—you know, I just have to be really candid. I think over the next—particularly heading up to the election, Iraqis are going to be increasingly focused inward on their internal issues and internal politics and our hope is that after those elections with a new government up we will work with that government to really get at this problem.

Mr. Cicilline. And which leads to my final question. That is, is it clear to President Maliki and to the Iraqi leaders in general that the responsibility to defend their country is their responsibility and that their expectation should not be that the United States is going to fulfill that responsibility, that they have to—after a very long commitment from this country they have to take this responsibility of defending their country and doing the hard work of bringing stability and peace to their own country?

Mr. McGurk. Absolutely, and when General Austin was in Iraq last week, and I was in those meetings with him and Iraqi leaders, they all stressed four or five points.

First, they want all of our support to be under the strategic framework agreement, which is a permanent foundation. That means institutional, military to military. They want training support and we're talking about doing some training in Jordan or in the region.

They want intelligence support and they want to let us know when they feel that they need weapons or systems that we can help them supply. So that is what they want, and they also want advice and recommendations for how to actually plan effectively. They do not want us to be in the lead in this fight. It's their fight.

Mr. CICILLINE. Thank you. I yield back. Thank you, Mr. Chairman.

Mr. KINZINGER. Gentleman from Rhode Island yields back.

Chair recognizes himself for 5 minutes.

Mr. McGurk, thank you for coming in. We really appreciate it. I appreciate your service to your country and dealing with these very tough issues.

I'm, obviously, not very happy with what's happening in Iraq and I've been very clear that I thought the withdrawal from Iraq was one of the biggest mistakes, I think, historically that'll be shown that the United States has made in modern foreign policy.

So I'm going to express a lot of concern with that. It's not necessarily directed at you but it is directed at the decision by the administration.

I'm a Air Force pilot and I served in Iraq a number of times and I remember specifically going there in 2008 and still, you know, watching the environment and seeing people hunker down, in essence, as there was still a threat of terrorism but they were starting to emerge.

And I then I remember going in 2009 and seeing an Iraq that had completely turned around and actually as, you know, somebody there thinking hey, you know, we're serving a purpose here—we've brought freedom to people, kids are out playing soccer.

Even though most of our operations in some cases were directed against Iranian assets Iran is now—is known to be responsible for directly or indirectly the death of about half of the Americans in Iraq, including EFPs. And by the way, I might want to mention that we are now negotiating with Iran in terms of giving them their ability to enrich uranium.

I'll tell you another concern I had is I remember I was actually getting ready to fly a mission into Afghanistan back a few years ago when I heard the Senate majority leader from the other side of this building say that the war in Iraq was lost, and he still has his powerful position but he very quickly said that the war in Iraq is lost and it's time to withdraw all the troops.

And then President Bush made what I think is a very brave decision to not only not withdraw but to actually surge more troops and then we saw a great deal of success.

I think the reason it's important to revisit these decisions is not beating a dead horse but it's the fact that we're getting ready to face the same kind of decision in Afghanistan.

Are we a country tired of war and we're going to pull out and have to deal with this shameful thing that we've seen in Fallujah, the equivalent of that in Afghanistan now, or are we going to learn lessons from the past? And I think it's very important to learn those lessons.

I've got a question—a couple of quick questions. There used to be a policy in this country that anywhere al-Qaeda exists they should know that there's no safe haven. I think President Bush talked about that there's no safe haven for terrorists anywhere in the country.

We see in Iraq right now they in essence appear to be somewhat safe. Hopefully, the Iraqi Government can push against them. We see the same type of situation in Syria and I'm for intervention in Syria. I want to be very clear about that.

Has this—does this—is this a change in the administration from the Bush policy of no safe haven anywhere in the world and now we accept safe havens in Iraq because we just lost the political will to do anything or is it still kind of the Bush policy of no safe haven for al-Qaeda?

Mr. McGurk. First, Congressman, thank you for your service and I think particularly now everybody who served in Iraq and has experience there it's really time for us to have a constant ongoing dialogue because we can all bring our experience and relationships to bear at this very important moment.

Again, I can just speak to Iraq and in working with the Iraqis in terms of intelligence support and Hellfires and, as I mentioned in my testimony, we are confident that Iraq will deny al-Qaeda safe havens in western Iraq.

One of the reasons we believe we saw the convoys moving into Fallujah and Ramadi is because the Iraqis started hitting their camps and safe havens in the remote regions of western Iraq.

So I am confident, particularly as the Hellfire missiles and they develop even more sophisticated ability to deploy them and also with the Apache helicopters and with the other things we're able to do with our Iraqi partners, that al-Qaeda will not have safe havens to plan and plot in those areas and that's one reason, though, they're moving into urban areas because it's harder to root them out of those areas.

Mr. Kinzinger. Thank you, and I'd like to say too I have called for and believe that the United States should help the Iraqi Government in a limited way using air power—American air power to take out these safe havens because this Congress, this House, has passed a use of force agreement that says attack, basically, al-Qaeda and so I think we have the authority and we have the responsibility to do that.

Let me ask you one more brief question. Israel foiled and dismantled what the Israeli officials describe as an advanced al-Qaeda plot within their borders.

There's kind of this far war grand strategy with al-Qaeda and a near war grand strategy. The near war is co-opting, for instance, Iraq—you know, all those places.

The far war would be a threat to the U.S. homeland. Do you believe that the situation we're seeing in—and that it's the goal of AQI to be part of a far war strategy, a.k.a. an attack on the American homeland eventually?

Mr. McGurk. Again, my file is Iraq so I'm focused on Iraq. I would just——

Mr. Kinzinger. But, obviously, Iraq has huge implications for the homeland?

Mr. McGurk. Again, I think al-Qaeda is a real threat. If they're able to entrench in the heart of the Arab world it'll threaten our interests throughout—vital U.S. interests throughout the region.

Mr. KINZINGER. All right. Thank you. And, again, thank you for your service to your country. I appreciate that.

Chair now recognizes Mr. Vargas for 5 minutes.

Mr. VARGAS. Thank you very much, Mr. Chair. Appreciate it.

You know, I think for most Americans trying to keep score at home it's becoming very difficult to understand the situation.

I think a lot of the nations there become somewhat confused and complex. I mean, Iraq, Iran, Syria—it's all kind of running together and the issue of the Sunni-Shi'a discord and what's happening there.

But what is very, very clear, I think, is the terrible price that Americans have paid. As you know very well and, again, thank you for your service, I mean, the amount of sons and daughters that didn't come home alive, the number of parents—mothers and fathers that didn't come home alive and those that did that brought the demons home with them that will haunt them and their families for the rest of their lives, I mean, we've paid a terrible price.

And so, I mean, today I heard even from some on the other side they were saying, you know, to hell with it. Let them kill themselves. You know, let them just fight it out—what should we be doing there. I don't hold that same feeling.

I think that, you know, the price that we paid has to mean something and the sacrifice that these people made, our brothers, our sisters and our country and the price that they paid has to mean something at the end of the day and we should do as much as we can.

I mean, I personally am very concerned about the Christian community. You know, the Christian community has been slaughtered. I mean, the Christians that we saw killed on Christmas—you know, very unified attacks against Christians, 37 murdered. The Chaldean community before the war was about 1 million Chaldean Christians.

Now, I think, there's less than half, maybe even a third of that. We're very thankful in San Diego that many Chaldeans have been able to come to San Diego and a great community that's forming there and continues to form.

But I'd like to hear from you what we can do and what we should do and what we're not doing to help not only the Christian community but especially the Christian community but other communities as well. I mean, what else should we be doing?

Mr. McGURK. Congressman, thank you.

I've visited the Chaldean community in Michigan and I would welcome the opportunity to come to your district also to visit the community there.

Mr. VARGAS. You're invited, then. Love to have you.

Mr. McGURK. And these extremist groups, as I mentioned, are threatening Christians, Muslims, everybody in the region. It is a phenomenon throughout the region that is a regional problem, and one thing we're trying to do is work with the Christian leaders in Iraq to make sure that they have the resources they need from the central government and also the Kurdish regional government and making sure that their areas are as secure as possible.

46

In Iraq, the Chaldeans and other Christian minority groups are located in the Nineveh Plains. There is an al-Qaeda extremist presence south of there.

We are working to try to make sure that local people, Christians in that community, have the resources to protect themselves and to police their own communities and we've made some progress in that area over the last 6 months.

In the north in Erbil and the Kurdish region, when I was in Iraq a few months ago and I met, as I mentioned earlier, with Archbishop Warda—the head of the community there—and linked him up with the Prime Minister of the Kurdish region to talk about schools for the community and making sure that they're getting the resources they need from the Kurdish regional government.

So what we can do as a neutral player in Iraq with relationships between everybody, because we've been there for 10 years and we're seen as a neutral player—one of the very few—is try to make sure that the connections are made between the governments—provincial, regional and national—so that the Christian and minority communities have the resources they need to protect themselves but also for schools and for children and everything else.

Mr. VARGAS. Now, I do have to say, though, I've heard from many that the central government—they claim that the central government is not doing much at all to help the Christians. In fact, just the opposite—that they leave them exposed, that their churches are exposed, that the schools are exposed.

I mean, could you comment on that, that they haven't been doing enough and not nearly enough to protect the Christian community and especially the churches?

Mr. MCGURK. Since a series of church bombings, if I recall correctly in 2009 or 2010, the Iraqis have really buttressed the protection of Christian sites in Iraq. But as you mentioned, there are still attacks on these sites.

Mr. VARGAS. The Christmas attacks, I believe, killed 37 Christians.

Mr. MCGURK. That's right, and I have found the Prime Minister, when you discuss this issue with him, fairly emotional about it, wanting to protect Christians, just like everyone else in his country and looking for ways to do that.

But it's something that, again, we're going to have to keep focusing on. But I think the more communication the better from the Christian community—Iraqi Christian community here in the U.S. who have deep ties back into Iraq and with us.

There's a lot that, if your constituencies tell you something they're seeing and you can let us know we can—we can work those problems.

Mr. VARGAS. Thank you.

I yield back. Thank you, sir.

Mr. KINZINGER. Thank you, Mr. Vargas.

Chair recognizes Mr. Yoho for 5 minutes.

Mr. YOHO. Thank you, Mr. Chairman.

Mr. McGurk, thank you for your testimony. I feel like you've been sitting there a long time. You might need to get up and stretch. But I appreciate your endurance.

What are our military assets in Iraq and are they purely advisory and, if so, how many? Can you divulge that or——

Mr. MCGURK. We have, under our Embassy—under the chief of mission and Ambassador Beecroft, the Office of Security Cooperation which works very closely with the Iraqi military.

The numbers ebb and flow but it's about 100 personnel and they do everything from advising to running the FMS programs to making sure that that is running efficiently, and a very small contingent of half a dozen or so of our special operators who train some of the higher end special operators as a training component. That's all done under the Embassy chief of mission and the Office of Security Cooperation.

Mr. YOHO. All right. So we have a very small footprint as far as——

Mr. MCGURK. Yes.

Mr. YOHO [continuing]. Americans there. What can be learned from how we left Iraq and applied to the draw down in Afghanistan so we don't make the same mistakes or repeat what we've done there so that we've got the benefit of the effort we put in there, you know, that both sides benefit from this?

What do you see that we need to do different? If you could write—rewrite a post draw down of troops in Iraq, especially with the announcement which I think was wrong, of the end date announced, what would you do differently so that we don't repeat that in Afghanistan?

Mr. MCGURK. I think, Congressman, you'll have to forgive me. I think I'm—when I'm out of government I might look back and work with historians on the history or also make comparisons to Afghanistan. But right now, I'm focused on the situation at hand and trying to protect our interests as we face right now.

Mr. YOHO. All right. Let me switch over to a different topic.

I've talked to many veterans that have fought both in Iraq and Afghanistan and we've talked to members of the Iraqi Government, and what they have said is that we have come to a stalemate between the Iraqi military or the Iraqi men and our military and a stand-off. In the meantime, countries like China, Japan, South Korea are going in there, building infrastructures and trading.

Would it not benefit us to put more effort into that so that we do have economic trade and that way we can help them build an economy where they own more of trying to solve this problem?

I know they're—I know they're working hard on it but if we can help build that infrastructure and work with developing trade.

Mr. MCGURK. I agree with you 100 percent, and while the focus of this hearing has been the al-Qaeda threat and the rising extremist threat our policy, as I discussed last time, is really multifaceted and one of them is developing economic ties and economic relationships.

We do advocacy for U.S. companies. We are proud that Boeing has signed a major contract with Iraqi Airways to be the backbone of the—of Iraqi Airways.

We're proud that Hill International Company, a U.S. company, has contracted with the provincial government of Basra to lead the effort there to try to modernize Basra in a very long-term 5- to 10-

year project. I can go through a number of companies—General Electric and others who are doing very well in Iraq.

But I agree with you, we need to get the private sector involved and invested in Iraq and there are a lot of opportunities, particularly in parts of the country that are very secure.

Mr. YOHO. That's where I'd like to, you know, help focus our foreign policy and that's why I was asking you if you could rewrite that.

With Fallujah, do you think the Iraqi Government can control Fallujah and defeat the ISIL? Do you feel like they can go in there, they have the willpower or the assets to do that?

Mr. McGURK. As I said in my testimony, I think without the support of the local population it'll be extremely difficult. That's a lesson that we learned in Iraq.

Mr. YOHO. All right. What about with—you were talking about the backbone—U.S. is the backbone of the Iraqi military. Were you meaning with our military assets?

Mr. McGURK. With equipment and training the Iraqis consistently look to us to be their primary supplier and primary supporter.

Mr. YOHO. Okay. And then Chairman Royce was asking about where the foreign fighters were coming from and I know a lot of them are coming from Europe. Is there any estimate how many are coming from the U.S. that go into Syria, then go over to Iraq?

Mr. McGURK. I don't have those numbers. I'd have to get—I'd have to go to the intelligence community and get back to you with those numbers.

Mr. YOHO. All right. Thank you.

Mr. Chairman, I yield back. Thank you.

Chairman ROYCE. Thank you, Mr. Yoho.

We go now to Mr. Collins of Georgia—Doug Collins of Georgia.

Mr. COLLINS. Thank you, Mr. Chairman. I appreciate the opportunity and thanks for answering a multitude of questions.

I want to turn back a little bit that was asked earlier about the elections and, really, from serving in Iraq and back in '08, as my colleague has as well, the understanding of the relationship between the Sunni and Shi'a is something that is—I think there's a huge mistrust that goes back generations. There's a multitude of issues there, and it looks like the current government has done very little to really relate with that or work on that relationship.

Experts in Iraq have talked about al-Qaeda in Iraq, Islamic State of Iraq some and increasingly building the alliances with Sunni tribal leaders, and has adjusted its message in 2013 to try and win more Sunni political support. How would that translate into the next round of Iraq elections?

Can we see—really see a move from Shi'a to Sunni and what does that mean for the region, and then answer that and then I want to talk about Iran's possible influence there as well. And I want to—just speak to the elections at this point.

Mr. McGURK. Thank you. First, Congressman, thank you for your service and it's a very important question—an insightful question.

This election coming up is going to be pivotal and also extremely interesting. The first national election in December 2005 there were really three main lists people could vote for. There was a Shi'a bloc, a Sunni bloc and a Kurdish bloc.

The 2010 elections there was a little bit more choice, really—two Shi'a blocs, the Sunni parties were under one main list also with some Shi'as, kind of a cross sectarian list, and then the Kurds.

This election everything is really fractured so you have about four Shi'a lists, you have three Sunni lists and even the Kurds are running on four different lists. So what's going to happen out of those results are going to be a number of different permutations in terms of forming governments and forming coalitions.

So the hope is that this election will give rise to the more possibility of cross sectarian kind of issue-based politics emerging. As difficult as that is going to be, if you look at the candidate list and the coalitions there is that possibility there.

But as I mentioned earlier, what al-Qaeda does very effectively is targets the fault line which has existed for 1,400 years, targeting symbolic areas and trying to increase fear in particularly the Shi'a population, which just rises the sectarian debate and discourse in the country.

So on the positive side, you have an election that's shaping up with a number of different choices, kind of number of different lists which will allow for cross sectarian coalitions. On the negative side, you have extremists who are trying to incite and inflame the sectarian dimensions in the country.

Mr. COLLINS. And I think that's sort of what we're heading in here and looking at, especially with the Iran influence in Iraq, the Shi'a population, and Iran's influence in one is what we're seeing there.

There's also the reports that, you know, I've read and others with dealing with the rest of the Arab world—Sunni Arab world—having to deal with this dynamic of Iran and Iraq and what's going on there.

Do you see or is there a sense that there is more push in the Shi'a with the Iran influence there and especially with everything else we've talked about here? Not encouraging discourse maybe is the best way to put it.

Mr. McGURK. Yeah. We've seen—if I could say, you know, 2011 and 2012, and I described in my written testimony this kind of low boil stage of insurgency, Shi'a militias and the most maligned Iranian influence were unable to really gain much traction because the violence was at this low boil.

As the al-Qaeda attacks went up this year, we've seen an increase in Shi'a militia activity, which has also given an inroad to the most nefarious Iranian activities.

So this is something that we continue to have to work with Iraqi not only political leaders but civil society leaders and everybody to try to isolate those most extreme groups.

Mr. COLLINS. And I appreciate it because I think and, really, what we look at and it's been mentioned, you know, several times here is we look at the world of Iraq right now and the issues of Fallujah and the Anbar region and then the price that we paid in those areas that are continuing.

We've got to maintain pressure on this administration in Iraq, whether it would be the protection of those that are at Camp Liberty to Ashraf, the other things. This is not something that this congressman is going to let go.

We got to continue this process. We owe that, in a large sense, to what happened there. So I think, really, in these elections that's the concern that I would express to Maliki is you've got to do the process of working to sustain your own country without the division and I think that's what we're expecting.

When we see stuff like what happened at Fallujah, when we see this action it tells me that maybe we're spending too much time doing other things and not doing the things that will keep that country, you know, on a path toward a sustainable future.

So I appreciate, and with that, Mr. Chairman, I yield back.

Chairman ROYCE. Thank you. Thank you, Mr. Collins.

We go now to Mr. Weber—Randy Weber of Texas.

Mr. WEBER. Thank you.

Mr. McGurk, you were last here in November. There's something—I think it's been 78 days as we count and with Iran fostering all of the unrest over in Iraq there's been 312 executions. If you divide that out it's one every 6 hours. It is four a day, 120 a month, hence, the 312 in 78 days.

It's been 78 days since you were here. We have a regime in Iran that is built on sending terror throughout its own citizenry and, of course, exporting it into Iraq. How many more executions do you think is acceptable before we take the Iranian regime to task over their executing their own citizens?

Mr. McGURK. I can address that from the Iran standpoint. Again, the human rights situation in Iran is quite despicable.

We have seen President Rouhani and Foreign Minister Sharif talk about wanting to make inroads and improve the human rights situation but, quite frankly, we have yet to see them make inroads in that area.

Mr. WEBER. So really, I mean, we need to be—we need to really be focused on this, even in our negotiations with or, I should say, the administration's negotiations over relaxing the sanctions because they don't—you know, we're getting played for fools, quite frankly.

I want to—I know that you're here to testify about al-Qaeda in Iraq so I have a question for you. The residents of Camp Liberty—are they as dangerous as al-Qaeda?

Mr. McGURK. No. No, certainly not.

Mr. WEBER. Okay. And yet and we promised them that, did we not, that we would protect them and that we would take care of them back during the conflict when they were repatriated, so to speak, to the camp?

Mr. McGURK. There were agreements between our kind of military commanders at the time when we moved into Iraq at Camp Ashraf.

Mr. WEBER. Right, and you're aware of how many of them have paid a terrific price with their lives to live there under the agreement that we made?

Mr. McGURK. I am, sir. Yes.

Mr. WEBER. Okay. And you're aware that they're basically having to live in graves now—we're not getting T-walls, the protection installed that they used—we had? I mean, it's just unbelievable the paper thin walls that they're living in and the attacks that are coming from outside. You're aware of that?

Mr. MCGURK. Yes, sir. And as I said, I was at the camp this month and talked to the residents about what it's like to live in a trailer when colleagues of yours are being killed by rockets in trailers. It's something that many of us can recall quite clearly.

Mr. WEBER. Well, good news and bad news. The good news is most of them, as I understand it now, are not living in trailers. The bad news is they've had to dig out a 3-foot wide by 6-foot grave, basically, and live in it to avoid the rocket attacks.

How long should—how long does that have to go on? Should we not be pressing for, A, to get them out of the country and, at best, while we're working diligently on that should we not be getting them protection? How much longer do you estimate that going on?

Mr. MCGURK. As I said earlier, we need to do everything we can to get them—to get them out of the country.

Mr. WEBER. Well, you were here 78 days ago. Has their situation improved?

Mr. MCGURK. Some more of them have been able to relocate to Albania, which—and we have to thank the Albanians for being very gracious for taking about 210 residents into Albania.

Mr. WEBER. Okay.

Mr. MCGURK. And we wish there were more countries willing to do the same.

Mr. WEBER. I'm told your comments earlier—I was—I was late from another hearing—that you made comments that the T-walls are currently being installed.

Mr. MCGURK. That was the information that I received this morning——

Mr. WEBER. Okay.

Mr. MCGURK [continuing]. That they would—the T-walls would begin moving in again today or tomorrow.

Mr. WEBER. Would you be interested to know that we've had cell phone communication from the residents inside the camp and that's not the case?

Mr. MCGURK. All I can say, Congressman, my understanding was there was a decision made this morning to begin moving T-walls back into the camp. Whether or not that's actually started or not, I don't know.

But I can assure you, based upon the information I've received that we will follow up and if in fact T-walls are not being moved into the camp that will be a very serious matter and I will follow up with you as soon as I receive the information.

Mr. WEBER. How soon?

Mr. MCGURK. I can follow up with you in the next 48 hours to make sure that T-walls are moving back into the camp.

Mr. WEBER. Okay. And is there a third party verification? Because when the Iraqi Government—I'm sorry, they just—for me they don't have a lot of credibility. It's almost as if the residents of Camp Liberty are the enemy and not the victims that they are.

Is there a third—I mean, surely you're not saying that you're going to call them and they're going to say of course?

Mr. MCGURK. No, no, no. We will—we will talk to our colleagues at the United Nations mission in Iraq and the deputy there, George

Bustin, who is at the camp regularly and he will be able to verify with eyes on whether or not.

Mr. WEBER. As we watch Iraq descend, I hope you make it an extreme priority to get them out.

Mr. McGURK. We will do so. Thank you.

Mr. WEBER. Thank you.

Chairman ROYCE. Thank you.

Well, let me just begin by thanking Mr. McGurk for—not just for your time this morning but for your work on this issue. As you know—as you can tell, this committee is extremely concerned about the resurgence of al-Qaeda, the impact that's going to have there in Iraq, the impact it's going to have on the region and, of course, even here to us in the United States.

So we thank you for that. We look forward to continuing to work with you on the concerns that we have in the House. There is one other issue that I meant to raise with you and that's just turning for a moment to discuss the inclusion of the Kurdish Democratic Party and the Patriotic Union of Kurdistan and the PATRIOT Act's Tier 3 designation—terrorist designation.

My understanding is that this has become a sort of catch-all designation that has inadvertently mislabeled the KDP and the PUK as terrorists even though they have been a stabilizing force in the region and consistently loyal to the United States for decades.

As al-Qaeda and associated groups expand across the Middle East and beyond, it seems like a good time to take count of our remaining friends in the region and maybe take a look at this inappropriate designation and recognize that that's harming our very important relationship with the Kurdish people.

So would the administration be supportive of a legislative solution to this issue that would exclude these Kurdish groups from the Tier 3 designation?

Mr. McGURK. Mr. Chairman, thank you for asking that question and for allowing me to put our response on the record.

As you said, the Kurdish people, the PUK, the KDP have been among our closest friends in the region going back decades. We think they should be removed from this list as soon as possible. We think it is an imperative. We understand that it requires a legislative fix.

It is nothing that we can do by executive action alone and therefore we are 100 percent supportive of an immediate legislative fix to this problem and we look forward to working with you and the relevant committees in Congress to get that done.

Chairman ROYCE. Well, thank you, Mr. McGurk. We did have to get you on the record for that and the Senate is working on this with the House, and we very much appreciate once more your testimony here today.

Thank you, Members. We stand adjourned.

[Whereupon, at 12:10 p.m., the committee was adjourned.]

APPENDIX

MATERIAL SUBMITTED FOR THE RECORD

FULL COMMITTEE HEARING NOTICE
COMMITTEE ON FOREIGN AFFAIRS
U.S. HOUSE OF REPRESENTATIVES
WASHINGTON, DC 20515-6128

Edward R. Royce (R-CA), Chairman

February 5, 2014

TO: MEMBERS OF THE COMMITTEE ON FOREIGN AFFAIRS

You are respectfully requested to attend an OPEN hearing of the Committee on Foreign Affairs, to be held in Room 2172 of the Rayburn House Office Building (and available live on the Committee website at http://www.ForeignAffairs.house.gov):

DATE: Wednesday, February 5, 2014

TIME: 10:00 a.m.

SUBJECT: Al-Qaeda's Resurgence in Iraq: A Threat to U.S. Interests

WITNESS: Mr. Brett McGurk
Deputy Assistant Secretary for Iraq and Iran
Bureau of Near Eastern Affairs
U.S. Department of State

By Direction of the Chairman

The Committee on Foreign Affairs seeks to make its facilities accessible to persons with disabilities. If you are in need of special accommodations, please call 202/225-5021 at least four business days in advance of the event, whenever practicable. Questions with regard to special accommodations in general (including availability of Committee materials in alternative formats and assistive listening devices) may be directed to the Committee.

COMMITTEE ON FOREIGN AFFAIRS
MINUTES OF FULL COMMITTEE HEARING

Day___*Wednesday*___Date_____*02/05/14*_____Room_____*2172*_____

Starting Time __*10:07 a.m.*__ Ending Time _*12:10 p.m.*__

Recesses __*0*__ (___`___to_____)(____to_____)(____to_____)(____to_____)(____to_____)(____to_____)

Presiding Member(s)

Rep. Edward R. Royce, Chairman Rep. Adam Kinzinger
Rep. Ileana Ros-Lehtinen

Check all of the following that apply:

Open Session ☑   Electronically Recorded (taped) ☑
Executive (closed) Session ☐   Stenographic Record ☑
Televised ☑

TITLE OF HEARING:

Al-Qaeda's Resurgence in Iraq: A Threat to U.S. Interests

COMMITTEE MEMBERS PRESENT:

See Attendance Sheet.

NON-COMMITTEE MEMBERS PRESENT:

None.

HEARING WITNESSES: Same as meeting notice attached? Yes ☑ No ☐
(If "no", please list below and include title, agency, department, or organization.)

STATEMENTS FOR THE RECORD: *(List any statements submitted for the record.)*

IFR - Rep. Poe
QFR - Lowenthal

TIME SCHEDULED TO RECONVENE _____
or
TIME ADJOURNED *12:10 p.m.*____

Jean Marter, Director of Committee Operations

HOUSE COMMITTEE ON FOREIGN AFFAIRS
Full Committee Hearing

Present	Member	Present	Member
X	Edward R. Royce, CA	X	Eliot L. Engel, NY
X	Christopher H. Smith, NJ		Eni F.H. Faleomavaega, AS
X	Ileana Ros-Lehtinen, FL	X	Brad Sherman, CA
X	Dana Rohrabacher, CA		Gregory W. Meeks, NY
X	Steve Chabot, OH	X	Albio Sires, NJ
X	Joe Wilson, SC	X	Gerald E. Connolly, VA
	Michael T. McCaul, TX	X	Theodore E. Deutch, FL
X	Ted Poe, TX		Brian Higgins, NY
X	Matt Salmon, AZ		Karen Bass, CA
X	Tom Marino, PA		William Keating, MA
	Jeff Duncan, SC	X	David Cicilline, RI
X	Adam Kinzinger, IL		Alan Grayson, FL
X	Mo Brooks, AL	X	Juan Vargas, CA
X	Tom Cotton, AR	X	Bradley S. Schneider, IL
X	Paul Cook, CA	X	Joseph P. Kennedy III, MA
X	George Holding, NC	X	Ami Bera, CA
X	Randy K. Weber, Sr., TX		Alan S. Lowenthal, CA
X	Scott Perry, PA		Grace Meng, NY
	Steve Stockman, TX	X	Lois Frankel, FL
X	Ron DeSantis, FL		Tulsi Gabbard, HI
X	Doug Collins, GA	X	Joaquin Castro, TX
	Mark Meadows, NC		
X	Ted S. Yoho, FL		
	Luke Messer, IN		

Insert for the Record
Submitted by the Honorable Ted Poe

Questions for the Record
Submitted by the Honorable Alan Lowenthal
To Mr. Brett McGurk

Question 1:

Which senior advisors recommended against Maliki doing a full scale assault against ISIS in Fallujah. Why did they do it? Can we trust Maliki to do what is necessary?

Answer:

In recent weeks, Deputy Secretary Burns, Ambassador Beecroft, GEN Lloyd Austin, CENTCOM Commander and I have all met with Prime Minister Maliki, and our message has been consistent with that of some senior Iraqi officials: to successfully expel ISIL from Fallujah will require the active support and participation of the local tribes. This also holds true in the overarching battle against extremism. Security operations can only have a sustained impact if fused with political initiatives and outreach to all of Iraq's political leaders and communities in order to address the complex challenges that remain in Iraq beyond the security realm.

Fallujah remains the scene of a tense standoff. Some tribes are ready and preparing to fight ISIL, others are working with ISIL (and forming "tribal councils" with the declared intention to fight the army), and more are on the fence, waiting to see which side is likely to prevail in the end. Local leaders in Anbar, in coordination with the Government of Iraq (GOI), are working to recruit more tribes to enter, clear, and hold Fallujah, while simultaneously ensuring civilians and families can leave the city.

This standoff will not last forever. The GOI has the responsibility to help local leaders secure the city and oust the militants now in control. Under the plan that is being developed by the GOI in coordination with local leaders, the army will seek to control outlying areas and cordon the city; tribal fighters will then seek to take the lead in securing populated areas, with military support when needed. We know from experience how difficult this will be, and U.S. military officers from the Office of Security Cooperation are in regular touch with their Iraqi counterparts to share lessons learned, offer advice, and make recommendations. During his recent visit to Baghdad, CENTCOM Commanding General Austin acknowledged the need to drive ISIL from Fallujah, but urged Iraqi commanders to use "strategic patience" as they accomplish this mission.

Question 2:

How many fighters have been recruited from the United States to fight for the al-Nusrah Front and ISIS?

Answer:

I am not able to provide numbers for you. The State Department does not track the activities of U.S. citizens abroad. Since U.S. citizens are not required to register their presence abroad, we do not maintain comprehensive lists of U.S. citizens residing overseas. We would refer you to the FBI for details pertaining to this question.

I can tell you, however, that we remain extremely concerned by the growing presence of foreign extremists among the Syrian opposition, including as members of the Islamic State of Iraq and the Levant (ISIL, also formerly known as the Islamic State of Iraq and Syria - ISIS) and the Nusra Front. These foreign extremists have very little stake in a negotiated solution to the Syria crisis that brings an end to the fighting and the establishment of a government that represents the aspirations of the Syrian people. The Department of State has engaged partners across Europe and the Middle East to urge steps to stem the flow of foreign extremists, including by enacting effective steps to enhance information sharing, law enforcement and border control measures and counter-radicalization programs.

Question 3:

With the rise of al-Qaeda both in Iraq and Syria what should be our role in Syria? Should we be more proactive in taking out Assad?

Answer:

The demand of the Syrian people for a new, democratic, open system of government for their nation will not be resolved on the battlefield. We firmly believe that the only solution to the crisis in Syria is political in nature. This is why we have invested a significant amount of capital, as have our allies and partners, and the United Nations, in creating a process with the goal of reaching a political solution to include the establishment of a transitional governing body. We expect that transitional governing body, which would have full, executive authority, including over the security services, will make rooting out violent extremism in Syria one of its primary goals.

Question 4:

Explain the relationship between ISIS and senior Al Qaeda leadership.

Answer:

The Nusrah Front and the Islamic State of Iraq and the Levant (ISIL, also formerly known as the Islamic State of Iraq and Syria - ISIS) began as franchises of al-Qa'ida (AQ). The groups vary in their methods and priorities: al-Nusrah has put greater priority on the toppling of Asad and working with other Syrian opposition groups, whereas ISIL has focused on a more regional agenda, with an aim to carve out an Islamic caliphate stretching from Baghdad to Lebanon. The split has been a central focus among global violent extremist networks. We believe it happened because of ISIL's unwillingness to follow Ayman al-Zawahiri's orders that it allow for al-Nusrah Front's continued independence within Syria and only fight in Iraq. Zawahiri has publicly distanced the AQ leadership from ISIL's unpopular actions against Syria's Sunni population, and it now appears that ISIL is conducting operations in Syria and Iraq entirely independent of any counsel or assistance from AQ core leadership.

Question 5:

In recent days, the Obama Administration has announced that it is expediting the delivery of U.S. defense articles to Iraq. If we are offering military assistance, how much are we pushing Maliki to make peace with the Sunnis within Iraq? Is it a condition of these sales that Maliki address the political sources of current violence? He has allowed Al Qaeda to have a foothold and has treated the Sunnis with indifference.

Answer:

We are working closely with Iraq to provide support for its fight against our mutual enemy, the Islamic State of Iraq and the Levant (ISIL). We continue to urge the Government of Iraq to fuse political and security efforts to address the immediate security situation while establishing a strategy to address long-standing Sunni grievances.

Security assistance is a key tool for building and shaping Iraq's defense capabilities and integrating Iraqi security forces into the region. Withholding security assistance during this volatile period would deal a serious blow to Iraqi efforts to defeat ISIL and weaken our strategic partnership with Iraq.

We continue to press the urgency of working with local Sunni leaders in the fight against ISIL in all of our engagements with Maliki, including meetings with the President in November and regular calls with the Vice President and during the recent visits of Parliament Speaker Osama Nujaifi and Deputy Prime Minister Saleh al Mutlaq, two prominent political leaders who represent Sunni majority areas of the country.

We have seen some progress from our efforts and are encouraged by the initial steps Maliki has taken to address legitimate grievances within the Sunni community and engage its members in the fight against ISIL. High ranking Iraqi Army officials have credited success in Ramadi to strong coordination between Iraqi Security Forces and local tribes – in addition to U.S. security assistance – and PM Maliki has agreed to incorporate tribes fighting AQI/ISIL into Iraq's security forces. In a February 9 press release, Maliki reiterated his support for the tribes and committed to their integration with local forces, while calling for reconstruction and reforms in Anbar province. He also recognized the Anbar tribes' integral role in defending the city of Ramadi against terrorist groups. In another push towards inclusion, PM Maliki recently pledged to hire these local tribe members as policemen in Anbar province. We are now actively encouraging all sides to follow through and engage in active dialogue with one another.

Regarding economic support, in January alone the GOI allocated $18 million for rebuilding projects in Fallujah and Ramadi; $17 million for direct humanitarian assistance; and $3.4 million for direct payments to tribal fighters. During Maliki's visit to Anbar province, the Iraqi government said it would increase these allocations further, and the cabinet on February 18 established a mechanism with national and local leaders to expedite the implementation and disbursement of funds to areas in need of assistance.

While recognizing the serious situation now confronting Iraq, we are encouraged by these efforts, and will continue emphasizing to Iraqi officials that the long-term strategy to defeat ISIL and achieving security and stability must include a political solution involving all of the people of Iraq.

Question 6:

Will the Administration put forth a repeal of the AUMF?

Answer:

The President has stated his intention to engage Congress about the Authorization to Use Military Force (AUMF) passed after the September 11, 2001, attacks to determine how we can continue to fight terrorists without keeping America on a perpetual war-time footing. The Administration is prepared to engage Congress and the American people in efforts to refine, and ultimately repeal, the AUMF's mandate.

With respect to the Authorization to Use Military Force against Iraq, the administration supports the repeal of the Iraq AUMF.